AF416602

Tales of Myth and Legend Series

Credits

Gods of Egypt: From Ra to Osiris / Mendoza Vester, Jorge

1st edition.- City of Santiago, Chile , 2023

www.historiayleyendas.com

First edition digital book

GODS OF EGYPT:
From Ra to Osiris

Contents

Introduction

Welcome to a fascinating journey through time, where the gods of ancient Egypt come to life on the pages of this book. Before delving into the rich mythology that captivated a millennia-old civilization, it is crucial to understand the context that shaped these divine beliefs.

Egypt, a land where the Nile River snakes like the backbone of civilization, witnessed a history intertwined with the magic of its gods and goddesses. On the banks of this majestic river, a civilization flourished that not only left footprints in the sands of time but also forged a pantheon of deities that defied human expectations.

The history of Egypt is woven with threads of powerful pharaohs, intricate hieroglyphics, and imposing monuments that stand as silent witnesses to a lost era. From the splendid construction of the pyramids to the complex social hierarchies, every facet of Egyptian life was imbued with a deep respect for the divine.

At the heart of this mystical narrative are the gods and goddesses who ruled the heavens, the earth, and the underworld. Their stories, so human in their emotions and conflicts, offer us a unique window to understand not only Egyptian mythology but also the very essence of a culture that has endured through the millennia.

Prepare to immerse yourself in a tale that unravels the mysteries of Osiris, the wisdom of Thoth, and the majesty of Ra. This book not only seeks to explore forgotten myths but also presents them in an accessible manner, providing a place where both the scholar and the curious can witness the Egyptian legends come to life.

Join us as we delve into the sands of time, where the ancient gods weave their stories, and discover the enduring and fascinating legacy of Egyptian mythology.

Ancient Egypt

Ancient Egypt was an ancient civilization that originated in the middle and lower course of the Nile River, with a history spanning over three millennia. It is believed to be one of the pillars of civilization.

The original name of the country, especially during the Old Kingdom, was Kemet, meaning "black land," referring to the color of the fertile silt that covered the Nile Valley during annual floods. This was in contrast to Deshret, the red land, representing the Sahara Desert that covers most of the Egyptian territory.

Although it has changed over the centuries, the area of ancient Egypt is generally considered to have extended from the Nile Delta in the north to Elephantine, at the first cataract of the Nile in the south. It also had control over the eastern desert, the Red Sea coastline, the Sinai Peninsula, and numerous oases scattered in the west. Historically, it was composed of Upper and Lower Egypt, situated in the south and north, respectively, before the formation of a unified state. During its greatest expansion, it ruled the Amorite kingdoms of Palestine and northern Syria, reaching the middle Euphrates, as well as the Nubian chieftaincies in Sudan, extending to Jebel Barkal at the fourth cataract of the Nile. Its cultural influence was significant in nearby communities and even in distant places like Cyprus, the Anatolian coast, and the Hellenic Peninsula.

The Egyptian civilization has existed for more than three thousand years. It began with the unification of some cities in the Nile Valley around 3200 BCE and is conventionally considered concluded in 31 BCE when the Roman Empire conquered and absorbed Ptolemaic Egypt, leading to the disappearance of the state. Although this event did not mark the beginning of foreign domination in Egypt, it caused a gradual change in the political and religious life of the Nile Valley, marking the end of the autonomous development of its cultural identity.

However, after victories over the Persians and Macedonians in the 6th century BCE and the Ptolemaic period, Egyptian influence began to decline gradually. After Christianity spread among Egyptians, Justinian I ordered the prohibition of the worship of the goddess Isis, putting an end to a religion that had persisted for more than four millennia. Nevertheless, the Egyptian language, known as Coptic, continued to be used, written in an alphabet derived from Greek, and the Egyptians fully embraced Christianity, especially the Monophysite doctrine.

A Coptic literature, with a Christian focus, emerged during that time, compiling myths, traditions, and beliefs of the ancient traditional religion. The replacement of Coptic by Arabic, as part of the Islamization of the country following its conquest, marked the end of the last remnants of Ancient Egypt.

Situated in northeastern Africa, Egypt boasts a unique combination of geographical features. It is surrounded by Libya, Sudan, and the Red Sea and the Mediterranean. The success of the Egyptian civilization was attributed to the Nile River, which allowed the exploitation of resources and provided a significant advantage over other countries. The fertile silt deposited on the banks of the Nile after annual floods enabled Egyptians to practice less labor-intensive agriculture than in other areas, allowing the population to dedicate more time and resources to technological, artistic, and cultural development.

The development of an autonomous writing and literary system, along with careful state control over natural and human resources, was primarily characterized by the irrigation of the fertile Nile basin and the mining exploitation of the valley and surrounding desert regions. It also involved the organization of collective projects such as large public works, trade with neighboring regions of East and Central Africa. The scribes, an elite socio-political and economic bureaucracy, were under the control of the Pharaoh, a semi-divine figure in a succession of dynasties ensuring the cooperation and unity of the Egyptian people within a complex system of religious beliefs. This bureaucracy was responsible for motivating and organizing these activities.

The Beginning of Egyptian Civilization

Origins of Egypt

Ancient Egypt is often envisioned as a land dominated by gods, kings, and priests. Its temples overflow with images of deities, and religion looms omnipresent in the remnants preserved from its three thousand years of civilization. Yet, little is known about the myths embodying their worldview. Written testimonies only exist from around 2000 BCE, although there are representations and pictorial allusions much earlier than this date: the kings of the II Dynasty depicted their conflicts in the struggle between Horus and Set.

Myths held less significance than the worship of gods, an essential state activity conducted in temples accessible only to the monarch and priests. If the worship was conducted properly, the country prospered. The divine service focused on the daily care of the images of the gods in their sanctuaries. The people rarely participated in the ceremonies, except as spectators during festivities where the deities "visited" each other and were carried in processions, sometimes by the river. The early temples were simple buildings surrounded by fences, but they increased in number and complexity as relationships among the older gods began to be established.

As these relationships became more complex, myths developed. Since a single version of each myth was not considered correct, their content adapted to various circumstances. For example, during the Late Period, the role of Set transformed, and he became an enemy of the gods, ritually annihilated.

Egypt Revealed by Herodotus

As the Greek historian Herodotus stated during his visit to Egypt in 450 BCE, Egypt was "a gift of the Nile." This was due to the annual inundation, the rise of the Nile waters in July that spread fertile mud across the lands, giving life to the country, which could not have existed without the Nile and its floods. This regularity, despite seasons of low or excessive flow – resulting in famines or disasters if the gods were angry or enraged – provided stability to ancient Egyptian ideas about life and death. The concept of Maat, the goddess embodying stability and law, governed all aspects of Egyptian life and religion.

The Egyptians believed in an afterlife, Jerneter or the Fields of Iahru (the Elysian Fields in Greek mythology), but they didn't locate it in the sky; rather, it was in the west, in the region of the setting sun. One of the titles of Osiris, the god of death, was the "First Lord of the Westerners." To access this otherworldly realm, two conditions had to be met: the preservation of the body – leading to the practice of mummification – and being judged as a just person (Maat beru, "of true voice") by the 42 gods in the Hall of Judgment, each of whom asked the deceased a question to which the true answer had to be "no." This ritual was known as the Negative Confession.

Within the mummy wrappings, a scarab made of hard green stone was included, bearing the inscription of Chapter 30 A or B of the Book of the Dead, titled "How my heart will not speak falsely against me in the Hall of Judgment." In some myths, other gods and goddesses appear, but they lack individual mythical backgrounds.

Since classical times in Greece and Rome, the religion of ancient Egypt has been a source of wonder and disbelief, even today. While the classical world had a vast pantheon of gods, with Zeus (Jupiter in the Roman world) at the helm, as well as ancient Egypt (with Amun-Ra leading the gods), it was the animal-shaped character of the Egyptian gods that caused unease.

Herodotus also noted that in Egypt, animals "must be considered sacred without exception," but he did not delve into the religious principles this implied.

Egyptian mythology indeed has a predominantly esoteric focus; there are not as many myths compared to those of the ancient Near East and later Mediterranean civilizations. Essentially, Egyptian myths deal with Creation, the Destruction of Humanity, the story of Isis and Osiris, the conflicts between Horus and Set, and the journey of the sun god Ra through the daytime sky and then through the 12 perilous hours of nighttime darkness to be reborn safely at dawn in the east.

Upper and Lower Egypt

The two regions that comprised the Egyptian state, Upper and Lower Egypt, held crucial importance in political and religious life.

Egyptian thinking was rooted in dualism: true unity didn't exist without subdivision, and before creation were the times "before there were two things." The country wasn't known by a single name but was referred to as "the Two Lands."

Horus was associated with Lower Egypt, and Set with Upper Egypt, while Nekhbet, the vulture goddess of Nekheb, and Uadjet, the cobra goddess of Buto, were linked to the monarchy.

In Upper Egypt, with significant centers such as Thebes, most evidence for reconstructing myths has been found. Still, some regions of Lower Egypt, like those around Memphis, are also of great importance.

According to archaeological evidence, the earliest settlers in Egypt established themselves around the 6th millennium BCE during the Neolithic period. The Egyptian population has relied on the Nile River since nomadic hunter-gatherers began inhabiting its banks during the Pleistocene. Objects and signs engraved on rocks along the Nile Valley and in oases represent traces of these early inhabitants.

In the 11th millennium BCE, a culture of grain gatherers was replaced by one of hunters, fishermen, and gatherers using stone tools along the Nile. In the southwest of Egypt, near the border with Sudan, human settlements were also established before 8000 BCE. According to geological evidence and climatological studies, climate changes began to dry up Egypt's hunting and grazing lands around 8000 BCE, gradually creating the Sahara Desert. As a result, tribes in the region gathered near the river, building small villages with an agricultural economy. In the eastern Sahara, in the 7th millennium BCE, there was herding and cereal cultivation.

Around 6000 BCE, organized agriculture and the construction of large populations had already emerged in the Nile Valley. In the southwest, people engaged in both construction and livestock farming. By 4000 BCE, lime mortar was already in use. The Predynastic period began with the Naqada culture.

Small settlements along the Nile flourished between 5500 and 3100 BCE during the Predynastic period. By 3300 BCE, Egypt was divided into two kingdoms: Upper Egypt (Ta Shemau) and Lower Egypt (Ta Mehu). The boundary between them was in the present-day region of Cairo, south of the Nile Delta.

The history of Egypt as a unified state begins with Menes (Narmer) around 3050 BCE, who united Upper and Lower Egypt and became its first king. For almost three thousand years, Egypt's religion, artistic creation, architecture, and social structure remained remarkably stable with little change.

During this time, the chronology of Egyptian kings commenced. Conventional chronology was used throughout the 20th century, ignoring subsequent revisions. Archaeologists often provide multiple dates and even various chronologies within the same work, leading to discrepancies among sources. Transcriptions of names are also available. Egyptology traditionally organizes the history of the pharaonic civilization into dynasties, relying on the epitomes of the Aigyptiaká (History of Egypt), written by the Egyptian priest Manetho.

Egyptian Society

Social structure in ancient Egypt was characterized by a hierarchy composed of three distinct levels:

- Pharaoh: Endowed with divine right, the pharaoh held all powers through the mediation of Horus.

- High Officials: This stratum included high priests and scribes, playing crucial roles in administration and spirituality.

- Common People: Encompassing peasants, artisans, and other groups, the common people constituted the base of Egyptian society.

Government and Politics in Ancient Egypt

Politics in ancient Egypt was marked by the organization into two kingdoms, Upper and Lower Egypt. However, around 3000 BCE, these two kingdoms were unified under a single monarchical, absolutist, and theocratic government.

- Monarchical: Egypt was ruled by a single king, consolidating power in the hands of a singular authority.

- Absolutist: The pharaoh, invested with divine authority, wielded absolute dominion over the kingdom, controlling all aspects of Egyptian life.

- Theocratic: The pharaoh, considered a god on Earth, personified the connection between the divine and the earthly.

The pharaoh, as the representative of the gods, claimed ownership over all of Egypt, including lands, crops, and trade. Among his various functions were the promulgation of laws, organization of the army, direction of religious life, administration of justice, and distribution of food to the population. Thus, the pharaoh not only governed but also embodied the stability and prosperity of the kingdom.

Organization of the State in Ancient Egypt

Absolute Power of the Pharaoh

Since predynastic times, the pharaoh, the incarnation of the god Horus on Earth, possessed absolute power over mortals. He was acknowledged as the owner of all of Egypt, including lands, crops, weapons, and the population. The pharaoh personally appointed viziers, priests, generals, and other high-ranking officials.

A manifestation of this absolute power of the pharaoh is art. The connection between art and political power is established from the dawn of history, where prevailing political ideas and positions serve as the main motivation for creating numerous artistic works with a clear propagandistic purpose.

Under this approach, the motive of the work stands as its essential foundation, determining parameters such as the distribution of images on the plane or surface used, the sizes of the images represented according to a hierarchical order based on the importance of the characters, and the use of certain forms as a synthesis of the concept to be conveyed.

The incorporation of art for propagandistic purposes was a common practice. During the New Kingdom, it was common to depict military campaigns towards Nubia, Syria, and Canaan in the successive expansions of the temples of Amun in Karnak. In this context, the consecutive pylons of these temples were adorned with reliefs showing the reigning pharaoh facing Asiatic or Nubian enemies.

Dynastic Law in Ancient Egypt

In Ancient Egypt, the concept of dynastic law was not based on a written legal structure but on the belief in the divinity of the pharaoh and the transmission of this status through the royal house's female line. Here are some key points related to dynastic law in the Egyptian context:

1. Transmission of Divinity:

- The pharaoh, believed to be the living Horus, upheld cosmic order (maat) and possessed absolute power.

- Divinity was transmitted through the women of the royal house, leading to marriages between siblings and even between fathers and daughters to ensure the continuity of divinity in the succession line.

- The heir to the throne was appointed co-regent and considered the bearer of the divine right.

2. Divine Will and Succession:

- There was no formal system of dynastic law, and succession to the throne was justified as "divine will." If a son of secondary wives became the heir, it was also considered a result of divinity.

- The coronation ceremony, held in Memphis, involved elevating the heir to the rank of a god and handing over the attributes of power, such as the crook and the flail.

3. Coronation Ceremony:

- During the coronation, the pharaoh was first crowned with the white crown of Upper Egypt, then with the red crown of Lower Egypt, and finally with a combination of both, symbolizing the unification of the Two Lands.

- He sat on a throne made of papyrus (symbol of the north) and lotus (symbol of the south).

4. Official Life of the Pharaoh:

- The pharaoh, considered a god and the son of gods, had the responsibility to perform worship and oversee all aspects of governance.

- Personally nominated priests and high-ranking officials, lived under strict etiquette, and fulfilled stifling obligations in his official life.

The succession system and the legitimacy of the pharaoh were rooted in the Egyptian religious worldview, where divinity and the continuity of cosmic order were fundamental.

Unification and Administrative Division

The unification of Upper and Lower Egypt during the time of Narmer marked the beginning of Egyptian culture, although administrative division persisted. Despite the merger, symbols of ancient duality were retained, with the double crown being a prominent example. The pharaoh, as the absolute owner of the land, had the right to its produce, although he sometimes granted lands to temples or individuals.

Distribution of Land and Control

The pharaoh could grant lands as payment for services or as conditioned rewards. Subleasing lands to peasants was common, and tax collection involved numerous officials. Frequent censuses were conducted, with individuals paying taxes in the form of labor, grain, animals, or artisanal products.

Priests

Priests played a central role in the religious and social life of Ancient Egypt, responsible for maintaining universal harmony, known as "maat." They were part of the ruling elite alongside scribes and the aristocracy. Here are some key aspects of scribes and priests in Egyptian society:

1. Scribes:

   - Scribes were essential in Egyptian administration, performing various functions such as recording trial proceedings, keeping warehouse records, overseeing taxes, drafting letters and contracts, and writing the laws of the pharaoh.

- Respected and admired, scribes had the opportunity to easily ascend socially after completing their studies in the "House of Life."

- They formed the backbone of the bureaucracy, being essential for the functioning of Egyptian administration.

2. Priests:

- Priests were delegates of the pharaoh, considered a living god. Their duty was to perform offerings, processions, and ceremonies to maintain cosmic order.

- Only the prayers and offerings of priests were deemed effective in maintaining maat, and they were depicted conducting ceremonies in the temples.

- Temples housed a large number of servants, including scribes, physicians, craftsmen, peasants, assistants, dancers, and musicians.

- The hierarchy of priests included readers, purifiers, prophets, and the High Priest of Amun, personally appointed by the pharaoh. The High Priest held significant political power and titles such as "Chief of the secrets of the sky" or "Chief of the priests of all the gods."

- Priests could marry and lead a life similar to wealthy citizens, but they had restrictions such as wearing white attire, regular depilation, and abstaining from sexual relations during worship periods.

- The figure of the priest was crucial in Egyptian society, and the priestly institution, considered directly created by the gods, endured throughout the three millennia of Egyptian civilization.

- The divinity of the pharaoh led to the great power of priests personally designated by him to represent him in worship.

Worship of the Gods and Religious Changes

In the heart of every temple, an Egyptian god was represented, embodied in a statue that was painstakingly attended to every day by the Pharaoh, or, in his absence, the priest. Amenhotep IV embarked on a radical reform, decreeing the abolishment of all gods in favor of a single deity, Aten, a manifestation of Ra. However, this foray into monotheism was short-lived; the pharaoh declared himself the sole intermediary between Aten and mankind, thus undermining the priesthood's standing. This met with strong opposition, and after Amenhotep IV's death, his son Tutankhamun, educated by the priestly caste, reinstated the worship of the entire pantheon.

For Egyptians, the ultimate aspiration after death was to become unified with the gods. This was achieved if the deceased passed the Judgment of the Dead and retained an incorruptible body to house their soul. Condemning bodies to water or fire, as with the accomplices in Prince Pentaur's attempted coup, was deemed as one of the most severe punishments.

Army: Organization and Equipment

Guarded by nature with the Nile and the desert, Egypt initially had little need for an organized army. However, with the Middle and New Kingdoms came uncertain borders and the necessity for military campaigns. In the Old Kingdom, the 'mesha' – a 'gathering of forces' – was mobilized as needed. Its duties included protecting borders, safeguarding maritime trade, and contributing to public works projects. In the First Intermediate Period, instability led local governors to form private armies and hire foreign mercenaries.

After repelling the Hyksos, the Eighteenth Dynasty of the New Kingdom undertook military campaigns that required a much more organized force. Specialized units like cavalry and chariots emerged, though their use was limited to the pharaoh and nobility. The infantry, the largest contingent, was organized into divisions, battalions, and companies.

Artistic representations have provided evidence that soldiers were armed with bows, arrows, scimitars, spears, maces, axes, daggers, and leather shields. Commanders were often of notable lineage, trained in officer schools, and were promoted based on their battlefield performance. Ordinary soldiers, a mix of natives and mercenaries, hoped to be rewarded with land which their descendants could inherit if they were eligible for military service.

Social Characteristics of the Army

The Egyptian society, known for its peaceful isolation and the influence of religious and state apparatus, was generally resistant to military enlistment. Joining the army was seen as a mark of low social status, with those in dire straits being the most likely to join, which meant the army was largely made up of foreigners.

This reluctance can be traced back to Egyptian culture, where the populace preferred to avoid military conflicts and focus on everyday life. Historical narratives align with this tendency, praising the glory of the pharaoh rather than detailing the experiences of the troops. The "Poem of Pentaur", which celebrates the battle of Kadesh in 1284 BC during the reign of Ramses II, exemplifies this, offering little insight into the day-to-day life of the soldiers.

Legal System in Ancient Egypt

In the Egyptian legal framework, the pharaoh was the central figure, officially responsible for enacting laws, dispensing justice, and maintaining public order - a concept known to the ancients as Maat. While no legal codes from Ancient Egypt have survived, judicial records suggest that Egyptian law was grounded in common-sense notions of right and wrong, favoring conflict resolution through compromises over adherence to a sprawling codex.

Local councils of elders, called kenbet in the New Kingdom, dispensed verdicts on minor claims and disputes. Serious cases, such as murders, substantial land transactions, and tomb robberies went to the High kenbet, presided over by the vizier or, in exceptional circumstances, the pharaoh. Plaintiffs and defendants had to represent themselves and swear to tell the truth. The state sometimes acted as both prosecutor and judge, using beatings to extract confessions and accomplices' names. Regardless of the offense's seriousness, court scribes documented complaints, testimonies, and verdicts for future reference.

Penalties varied from fines and beatings to facial mutilation or exile for minor offenses. For more severe crimes, execution was carried out by decapitation, drowning, or impaling the offender on a stake. Starting in the New Kingdom, oracles played a significant role in the legal system, deciding on both civil and criminal cases. The oracular deity would respond to yes-no questions regarding the morality of an issue. Carried by priests, the god would pronounce judgment by moving forward or backward or by pointing to a written answer on papyrus or an ostracon.

Economy in Ancient Egypt: The Wealth of the Nile

Ancient Egyptian life was deeply rooted in agriculture and livestock, with existence hinging on crops grown in the fertile lands irrigated by the Nile. An elaborate network of dykes, reservoirs, and irrigation channels spanned the arable land. Along the Nile banks, peasants toiled, producing a variety of cereals, most notably wheat, barley, and flax, with the grains stored in granaries for bread and beer production - staples in the daily diet.

The Cycle of the Nile

Agriculture followed the Nile's cyclical flow, with four seasons marking different phases: the "white pearl" denoted the river's rise, causing beneficial floods that deposited fertile silt; the "black pearl" marked the Nile's retreat, leaving behind black mud used for farming; the "emerald green" indicated the sprouting of crops; and the "red gold" symbolized the maturity of the fields.

The three seasons, Akhet (inundation), Peret (planting), and Shemu (harvest), defined farming activities. Akhet, from June to September, brought the flood and nutrient-rich silt to the banks. During Peret, from October to February, farmers waited until waters receded to plow and sow. Shemu, from March to May, was harvest time, with crops reaped using wooden sickles.

Variety in Production

In their gardens, Egyptians grew peas, lentils, onions, leeks, cucumbers, and lettuces as well as fruits like grapes, dates, figs, and pomegranates. Animal husbandry also played a critical role, with pigs, cows, sheep, goats, geese, and ducks being raised.

Trade and Prosperity

The plentiful food supply allowed Egyptians to engage in lucrative trade. They imported items such as incense, silver, and cedarwood from foreign lands. The Nile and the Mediterranean were key transport routes for these goods, contributing to Egypt's economic magnificence.

For roughly three millennia, Ancient Egypt enjoyed the status of the world's wealthiest nation, cementing its legacy as a thriving and economically vibrant civilization.

Economy and Agriculture in Ancient Egypt

Paintings in temples and tombs provide a glimpse into the dedicated efforts devoted to agriculture, which formed the backbone of the Egyptian economy. Pharaohs undertook costly canalization projects to control the Nile floods, essential for the fertility of the land.

The earliest canalizations date back to 3500 B.C., and by 1830 B.C., the first irrigation plan in Lower Egypt was established to ensure water reserves and enable cultivation during the dry season.

Initially, the land was royal property, but later donations led to a latifundia system with renewable annual leases. Economic stability maintained unchanged conditions for 3000 years: regardless of the harvest quality, 7 or 8 khar (86 liters of grain) per arura (0.25 hectares) had to be delivered to the landlord or the pharaoh's tax collector.

Crops included wheat, barley, flax, figs, onions, lettuce, and special attention was given to the vine for wine production, with details like origin, harvest year, and the vintner's name being cared for. Barley-made beer was also common and affordable.

Tree felling was strictly prohibited without royal permission, and fruit trees were often found in the private gardens of wealthy families. The Egyptian economy was entirely controlled by the State, overseeing agriculture, owning mines, distributing food, collecting taxes, and supervising foreign trade.

Agricultural Cycle in Ancient Egypt:

Life in Ancient Egypt was closely tied to the agricultural cycle, which was divided into three essential seasons: Inundation, Planting, and Harvest. The management of these seasons, especially the Nile floods, was crucial for the country's prosperity.

- Inundation:

After the fields were flooded and emerged, scribes measured and marked the boundaries. Subsequently, the head of the family plowed the land with a wooden plow pulled by oxen, while the rest of the family sowed the grain provided by State storehouses. Livestock was also released in the plot to bury the seed with their hooves.

- Planting:

While awaiting the harvest, irrigation channels were supervised, and livestock, including sheep, goats, oxen, and pigs, were cared for. The family participated in the harvest, with the man using a wooden and flint sickle, and women and children gathering the ears. The harvest was taken to the threshing floor, where it was threshed with the help of oxen, and then transported to public silos. The distribution of the harvest included officials, slaves, and laborers, and the surplus was stored to face possible hard times.

- Harvest:

During the inundation season, peasants took care of cleaning irrigation channels and participated in public works when summoned.

The vast majority of the population worked for the pharaoh, temples, and nobles, contributing to construction, home decoration, furniture and tomb manufacturing. Agriculture and water management were crucial for the stability and prosperity of Ancient Egypt.

Egyptian Economy: Storage and Exchange System

The wealth of Ancient Egypt relied on agricultural surpluses. After the harvest, products and livestock collected as taxes went to silos, which were fundamental in the Egyptian structure.

During the Old Kingdom, silos were conical with an opening at the top, and in the Middle Kingdom, they evolved into square buildings with roof openings that functioned as silos.

These silos served various vital functions:

- Accumulating reserves for times of scarcity.

- Paying wages to employees of the pharaoh, temples, or nobles responsible for the warehouse.

- Distributing seeds for the next planting.

- Selling surpluses abroad.

Managed rigorously by specialized scribes, warehouses were key to state intervention in economic affairs. Egypt lacked currency, and in everyday life, barter was practiced, valued in standard units. State machinery and surplus storage contributed to maintaining a stable economy without applying the laws of supply and demand, avoiding price differences and achieving remarkable economic stability without inflation for 30 centuries.

Quarry Workers and Miners in Ancient Egypt

Egyptian quarries, located in the desert, did not operate regularly but according to the needs of ongoing projects. The work of quarry workers was arduous: selecting blocks, transporting them, carving obelisks, and placing them could take months. Initially, they sought loose rocks of suitable size, although they also excavated galleries as needed. The method evolved with the creation of sloping roads to slide blocks on sledges, an innovative idea by overseer Mery. Quarry work was at the bottom of the craft scale, and many were prisoners of war.

The work of miners was even more challenging. To extract minerals, they heated the rock and pounded it along the vein. Fragments were taken from the mine galleries to be washed and transported. Since the mines were in the desert, and many miners were prisoners of war, mistreatment and water scarcity were common, making the miners' lives extremely difficult.

Trade, Routes, and Commercial Expeditions in Ancient Egypt

Breadth and Variety in Commercial Transactions

The commercial activity of the ancient Egyptians went beyond simple commodity exchange; it encompassed expeditions aimed at enriching royal treasuries with ornamental goods, jewelry, and surprisingly, the sale of slaves, as well as the disposition of administrative or service positions in temples.

The Shutiu: Commercial Agents

In Ancient Egypt, the shutiu played a crucial role as commercial agents, conducting buying and selling transactions in the service of pharaonic institutions such as temples, the royal palace, and large crown estates. These intermediaries were not limited to selling to institutions but also traded slaves, both to individuals and in independent transactions for their own benefit.

Balat: Operating Base in the Sahara

Archaeological evidence in the ancient city of Balat, located in the heart of the Egyptian Sahara, reveals that this town served as an operating base and supply point for commercial expeditions sent by the pharaohs to the heart of Africa in the late third millennium B.C. Through about 200 clay tablets and numerous inscriptions, it has been documented that these expeditions, consisting of approximately 400 men, set sail from the Dakhla Oasis with the aim of obtaining a pigment. This valuable resource, once acquired, was transported back to the Nile Valley by caravans.

The Route to the Heart of Africa

The commercial route was traced from time immemorial, evidenced by deposits of jars distributed every 30 kilometers in the desert, extending to Gilf el-Kebir at the southwestern end of Egypt. Although the exact extent of the route remains a mystery, the most plausible hypothesis among experts suggests that it extended to the Lake Chad area. This bold trans-Saharan trade not only highlights the economic sophistication of the ancient Egyptians but also their ability to explore and establish connections in vast regions of the African continent.

Achievements of Ancient Egypt:

1. Topography and Construction:

Developed advanced skills in topography to determine the exact position of points and distances between them, especially applied in the construction of the pyramids.

Invented mortar, a significant contribution to construction engineering.

2. Irrigation and Agriculture:

Built irrigation channels to harness the El-Fayum lake, turning the area into the main grain producer in the ancient world.

Utilized the natural lake of El Fayum as a reservoir to regulate and store water for use during dry seasons.

3. Resource Exploitation:

Since the first dynasty, exploited turquoise mines in the Sinai Peninsula.

4. Contributions to Medicine and Mathematics:

Created papyri like the Edwin Smith and Ebers Papyri, containing advanced medical knowledge and representing the earliest evidence of traditional empiricism.

Developed a decimal system and complex mathematical formulas, evidenced in the Moscow Papyrus and the Ahmes Papyrus.

5. Writing and Language:

Invented their own writing system: hieroglyphics, around the fourth millennium B.C.

6. Advances in Glass Manufacturing:

Developed glass manufacturing remarkably, as evidenced in numerous everyday use and ornamental objects discovered in tombs.

Remains of an ancient glass factory have been discovered.

7. Sailing Navigation:

Around 3500 B.C., invented sailing navigation, being the first application of non-animal energy to locomotion.

Used this invention exclusively for about 2100 years before the Phoenicians documented its use around 1400 B.C.

The civilization of Ancient Egypt left an impressive legacy in various areas, from engineering and science to writing and navigation, significantly contributing to the advancement of humanity.

Administration and Finance in Ancient Egypt

Administrative Organization

Egypt was structured into various sepats, equivalent to provinces or nomes in Greek, for administrative purposes. This division has its roots in the predynastic period (before 3100 B.C.), when nomes were autonomous like city-states, preserving their peculiarities for over three millennia. In total, the country was divided into 42 nomes, with 20 belonging to Lower Egypt and 22 to Upper Egypt. Each nome was under the rule of a nomarch, a provincial governor invested with regional authority.

Taxes and Tax System

The Egyptian government applied various taxes, paid in kind, through labor, or goods, as there was no standardized currency. The Tyaty (vizier) was the figure responsible for overseeing the tax system on behalf of the pharaoh through his department. The vizier's subordinates had to keep reserves and forecasts updated. The tax contribution varied based on occupation and income: peasants or landowners paid with agricultural products, artisans with a portion of their production, and similarly, fishermen, hunters, among others.

Public Work and Obligations

The state required each household to provide one person for public work for several weeks each year. These tasks included the construction and cleaning of channels, the building of temples or tombs, and even mining (only if there were no prisoners of war available). Hunters and fishermen contributed their taxes through catches from the river, canals, and desert. Affluent families had the option to hire substitutes to fulfill this civic duty.

This tax system, although based on the direct contribution of goods and services, demonstrated Ancient Egypt's ability to organize and sustain a complex administrative and financial machinery that allowed for prosperity and the maintenance of civilization over millennia.

Customs of Ancient Egypt

The customs of Ancient Egypt were rooted in daily routines, agriculture, and basic needs, all influenced by the vital presence of the Nile River. The Neolithic revolution along the Nile included gathering, animal domestication, and the observation of the abundant grass production in the silt of floods. This environment led to the development of an irrigation system, fostering an economy based on storage, which, in turn, promoted advances in science and art, such as writing, geometry, algebra, and astronomy.

Mummification and Beliefs in the Afterlife

Ancient Egyptians believed in life after death, where the body and spirit played distinct roles. The mummification process was essential to preserve the body and facilitate the transition to the future life.

The spirit consisted of three principles:

1. Aj (The Immortal): Represented the divine essence and left the body after death to join the gods.

2. Ka (Vital Energy): Continued to live a fictitious existence in the sarcophagus, sometimes represented by servant figurines called "Ushebti," intended to assist the deceased in tasks ordered by the gods.

3. Ba (The Spiritual): Left the body during the day but returned at night to avoid being devoured by evil spirits. It was represented as a bird in some versions of the Book of the Dead and symbolized the penetrating mind in connection with divinity.

The belief in immortality and life after death was also related to the desert, where corpses were buried. This environment possibly played a crucial role in the Egyptian conception of transcendence and eternity.

Roles and Family Dynamics in Ancient Egypt

In Ancient Egypt, family structure and gender dynamics played distinct roles in society. Here are some key aspects related to family in that context:

Role of Women:

- Egyptian women maintained their name and a certain degree of independence, engaging in various labor activities such as midwifery, weaving, or managing households, and collaborating in their husbands' businesses.

- Upon marriage, they gained status and could have roles as administrators of the estate (nbt pr). High-class women were depicted with lighter skin tones in paintings, indicating their status and access to cosmetics.

- Attention was given to physical appearance, especially hairstyles and makeup, symbolizing status and possibly purity and beauty.

Marriage:

- Marriage typically began when the couple decided to live together, usually at 12-14 years for women and around 16 for men. It did not require official sanction and was formalized with a private contract detailing each person's assets.

- Monogamy or polygamy were practical decisions and did not have significant legal or moral implications. The decision to have another wife could influence the distribution of assets and rights between the wife and children.

Divorce:

- Divorce was also a private matter and could be initiated by either spouse. Reasons ranged from adultery to infertility or even the physical appearance of the wife.

- If assets were detailed in the private contract, the wife could recover what was hers. Otherwise, she had the option to return to her parents.

These family dynamics reflected flexibility and pragmatism in marital relationships in Ancient Egypt, where legal and moral issues were considered practical and private matters within the family sphere.

Sexuality:

- There was notable sexual freedom in Ancient Egypt, evident in writings and fashion of the time. In its early stages, both women and men, excluding royalty, could go topless. In certain professions, like butchers, sailors, and servants, nudity was common.

- Relationships were not strictly controlled, and incest was frequent in the royal family. While adultery by women was not punishable, there are recorded cases of punishment, such as stoning, in some papyri.

Considerations about Menstruation:

- The only significant sexual taboo was related to considering menstruation as impure. Some workers were excused from work during the days when their wives had menstruation.

Children:

- Although children were desirable, contraceptives were used due to the high maternal mortality rate during childbirth.

- Children were cared for and educated without gender distinction, and many learned to read and write. The children of noble families attended the House of Jeneret school, also known as the queen's house.

These aspects illustrate the complexity and diversity of practices and beliefs related to family and sexuality in Ancient Egypt, where society displayed a mix of freedom and certain taboos, and the royal family often followed different norms than the rest of the population.

Clothing in Ancient Egypt:

Materials and Types of Fabrics:

- Initially, various fibers from reeds and rushes were used in addition to linen, which later became widespread due to the belief in its purity.

- Four types of fabrics: royal linen, fine utility fabric, subtle fabric, and smooth fabric. The preferred color was white, with some patterns on the edges.

- Men wore a short skirt called schenti, tied at the waist by two crossed ends.

Women's Attire:

- High-class women wore a kalasiris, a long, tight-fitting one-piece dress, held with two straps covering the breasts.

- They also wore a kind of short cape over the shoulders to protect themselves from the sun.

Changes in Clothing:

- In the Ptolemaic period, introduced by dynasties of Greek origin, a change in clothing occurred, especially for women, due to the concept of female immodesty. This led to women gradually covering more of their bodies.

- Workers usually went naked or wore loincloths, while working women wore loose clothing, although some also went naked.

Hair Removal and Personal Style:

- Royalty and royal scribes, both men and women, were always depilated all over their bodies. Some authors suggest that body hair distanced them from divinity, as it was considered a symbol of materialization.

- Although depilation was common, there were cases like that of the royal scribe Imhotep, depicted with a mustache or small beards.

Food in Ancient Egypt:

Worker's Diets:

- According to Herodotus, workers ate onions, garlic, bread, and beer, as they were paid in wheat and barley.

Variety in Diet:

- Paintings, reliefs, and offerings indicate that they liked birds, fish, and fruits. These foods are also represented on the Pharaoh's table.

- In tombs, preserved birds and fish have been found, as well as mummified beef. Meat was primarily obtained from sacrifices or as diplomatic offerings.

Egyptian Cuisine:

- Although dates were used for nutrition, Egyptian cuisine did not follow the typical Western order of appetizer, main course, and dessert.

- Egyptian tombs have been found with amphorae of honey and various fruit pits such as dates, citrus (possibly imported), and others.

House of Life in Ancient Egypt:

The House of Life, known in Egyptian as Per Anj, was an institution in Ancient Egypt that played advanced roles in teaching, library, archive, and manuscript copying workshop. These houses were exclusively reserved for scribes and priests and are known to have originated during the Old Kingdom. They were generally located in the royal palace or in a building within the temple area.

Each city of certain importance probably had its own House of Life, and there is evidence of these institutions in places like Amarna, Edfu, Memphis, Bubastis, and Abydos. In Amarna, the House of Life consisted of two main rooms and their annexes, including the residence of the institution's director.

The teachings in the Houses of Life were diverse and included medicine, astronomy, mathematics, religious doctrine, and foreign languages. The importance of learning foreign languages increased during the New Kingdom due to the cosmopolitanism of the era and Egypt's dominance over a vast area extending from Nubia to the Euphrates River.

Scribes working in these institutions held titles such as "Servants of Ra" or "Followers of Ra," associating their work with the Egyptian sun god Ra, considered the giver of life. Additionally, the Houses of Life were linked to Osiris, the god of rebirth. It was believed that the act of copying texts would contribute to the annual rebirth of Osiris during his festival.

Moreover, some Houses of Life also housed establishments that could be considered as sanatoriums, thus fulfilling functions related to health and well-being.

Jeneret House:

Jeneret House was an institution associated with the queen's residence in Ancient Egypt. Its primary function was the education of court ladies, covering various aspects but placing particular emphasis on instruction in music and dance. Young women learned to play musical instruments such as the harp, lute, and flute. Additionally, they were taught ritual dances whose melodies aimed to appease the deities, creating an atmosphere of harmony that delighted everyone.

Among the significant activities in Jeneret House schools were the making of dresses and the crafting of beauty and grooming utensils. For this, they had workshops for pottery, weaving, and carpentry. The hierarchy of Jeneret House was subordinate to the Great Royal Wife, and the administration included officials in charge of workshops, administrators, and servants. The institution's director held the title "Sehpset," meaning "the venerable." On the other hand, noblewomen belonging to Jeneret House carried the title "Royal Ornament."

Medicine:

Medicine in Ancient Egypt developed through the observation of the effects of plants on the human body, establishing a medical profession that gained prestige not only within the country but also abroad. They specialized in various areas of medicine, and Herodotus described the diversity of physicians and medical specialties in Egypt. Each physician dedicated themselves to treating a specific ailment, whether related to the eyes, head, teeth, abdominal region, or internal diseases.

Medicine in Ancient Egypt:

In Ancient Egypt, medical practitioners were known as sun-nu, translated as "men of those who suffer." These physicians used remedies combined with magical formulas, seeking divine intervention for effective treatments. Medical recipes from the time have been preserved in various papyri, such as the Ebers Papyrus, the Chester Beatty Papyrus, and the Hearst Papyrus, as well as in the tombs of some doctors.

Egyptian medicine encompassed a variety of practices, from the use of herbs and natural substances to surgical procedures. Additionally, seriously ill patients were interned in facilities near temples, with the belief that proximity to the gods would facilitate recovery. Given the importance of preserving the body for the afterlife, prosthetics were even placed on the corpses of those who had lost a limb during their lifetime.

The Egyptian administration intervened in the medical profession, turning physicians into officials. This provided them with guaranteed minimum income, in addition to what they could earn independently. There was a hierarchical system in the profession, culminating in the title "Chief of the Physicians of Upper and Lower Egypt," representing the pinnacle of the medical career in Egyptian society.

Egyptian medicine had specialists in occupational medicine, focusing on returning workers to their duties as quickly as possible, and this service was provided free of charge. Other notable specialties included gynecology, due to the importance of procreation, and surgery.

The teaching of medicine took place in the House of Life, linked to different temples. The abundance of medicinal herbs in the region contributed to the knowledge and practice of medicine, and Herodotus praised Egyptian physicians as the wisest in the world.

Architecture:

In Ancient Egypt, urban planning was not a common practice, and except for administrative centers or areas with specific purposes, there was no pre-planning in the construction of homes. Houses in Deir el-Medina, a city inhabited by builders of royal tombs, initially lacked foundations, but later expansions had stone foundations, forming walls with rows of bricks.

In general, there were no marked distinctions between rich and poor neighborhoods. Houses were mixed in layout and size, unless they belonged to individuals of high social class. Members of the same family usually lived in the same neighborhood. In Deir el-Medina, the city founded by Amenhotep I, family homes were surrounded by a wall. Its sudden abandonment during the reign of Ramses XI facilitated thorough study.

Deir el-Medina experienced its peak during the reign of Ramses II, relocating the capital from Thebes to the delta and abandoning the Theban necropolis. The arrangement of houses was organized around streets traversing the village, and trash dumped behind the wall provided valuable information about society through ostraca, fragments of pottery used for writing.

The earliest known dwellings date back to the Predynastic Period, constructed with adobe walls and roofs of logs covered with palm leaves and mud, similar to present-day houses. The construction technique remained unchanged, using sun-dried mud and straw blocks, fragile materials that left less significant archaeological remains compared to tombs and temples.

Houses of the Upper Class:

Models placed in tombs during the Middle Kingdom provide insight into the houses of the upper class in Ancient Egypt. Although direct representations decrease in the New Kingdom, papyri and paintings offer details about these residences. Additionally, the discovery of furniture, household items, board games, and tools sheds light on daily life.

Houses of the upper class were more spacious, and some kings and nobles combined two residences, resulting in larger properties with various rooms, courtyards, gardens, fountains, and orchards. Some even included bathrooms, with toilets depicted as stone containers with lids. These homes were adorned with frescoes, adding an artistic and aesthetic touch to their design.

A standard residence accommodated five to ten people, usually parents with children, sometimes from different mothers due to high mortality and frequent divorces. Houses were painted white, and rooms were arranged in a line, occupying between 40 and 120 m². Access was through a wooden door, and the interior arrangement included an altar in the first room, where lamps, jars, and braziers were also stored.

The main hall, illuminated by small windows protected by shutters or lattices, served as the central space. In it, there could be a cellar or ceramic containers. Stairs led to the cellar, and a door led to the rest of the rooms, which could be storage rooms and bedrooms. The kitchen was located in the street or in the backyard, which often contained an oven and a small grain storage. These details offer a fascinating glimpse into the organization and life in the residences of the upper class in Ancient Egypt.

Temples:

Temples played a fundamental role throughout Egyptian history, from its beginnings to the peak of civilization, and were present in most communities. They included mortuary temples to honor the spirits of deceased pharaohs as well as temples dedicated to patron gods, although the distinction between the two was blurred due to the close relationship between divinity and monarchy. While not primarily places of worship for the general population, state-sponsored temples served as abodes for the gods, housing physical images that acted as intermediaries and received offerings to sustain the gods and, consequently, the universe itself.

Temples were essential to Egyptian society, and vast resources were allocated for their maintenance, with contributions from the monarchy and large estates. Pharaohs often expanded temples as part of their duty to honor the gods, resulting in the construction of large temples. However, not all gods received dedicated temples, as some important deities in official theology had minimal worship, while various popular gods in local contexts were the focus of popular veneration, not temple rituals.

Early Egyptian Temples:

The first Egyptian temples were small and impermanent structures, but throughout the Old and Middle Kingdoms, their designs became more elaborate and increasingly built with stone. In the New Kingdom, a basic temple design emerged, evolving from common elements in earlier temples. This standard design included a central processional path leading through courts and halls to the sanctuary, where the temple god's statue resided. Access to this part was restricted to the pharaoh and the highest-ranking priest, symbolizing a journey from the human world to the divine realm. Beyond the temple building was the outer wall, with subsidiary buildings between them, such as workshops, storage areas, and a library housing sacred writings and mundane records, serving as a center of learning.

In theory, it was the pharaoh's responsibility to carry out temple rituals as the official representative of Egypt to the gods. However, in practice, ritual duties were almost always performed by priests. During the Old and Middle Kingdoms, there was no separate priestly class; instead, many government officials fulfilled this role for several months a year before returning to their secular duties. It was only in the New Kingdom that a professional priesthood became widespread, although most lower-ranking priests still worked part-time. All of them were employed by the state, and the pharaoh had the final say in their appointment.

With the growth of temple wealth, the influence of its priests also increased, sometimes rivaling that of the pharaoh. During the political fragmentation of the Third Intermediate Period (c. 1070-664 BCE), the high priests of Amun in Karnak even became effective rulers of Upper Egypt. Temple staff was not limited to priests but also included non-priests such as musicians and ceremony singers. Outside the temple, there were artisans, workers, and farmers who helped meet the temple's needs. All received their salaries from temple profits. In this way, large temples became significant centers of economic activity, sometimes employing thousands of people.

Rituals and Official Festivals:

Among the religious practices of the Egyptian state, various deity worship rituals and ceremonies related to divine monarchy took place in temples. These included daily rituals, such as the morning offering ceremony, where a high-ranking priest, occasionally even the pharaoh, would wash, anoint, and elaborate the statues of the gods before presenting offerings. Once the gods had consumed the spiritual essence of the offerings, the objects were distributed among the priests.

In addition to daily rituals, there were less frequent but numerous festivals, with dozens occurring each year. These festivals went beyond simple offerings to the gods and involved actions such as recreations of specific myths or the symbolic destruction of forces of disorder. Most of these events were probably celebrated only by priests and took place inside the temple. However, major festivals, like the Opet festival held in Karnak, involved processions carrying the god's image outside the sanctuary on a model boat to visit other significant sites, such as the temple of a related deity. Commoners gathered to witness the procession and sometimes received portions of the offerings given to the gods on these occasions.

Popular Religion:

Popular religion in ancient Egypt manifested more directly in the daily lives of individuals, contrasting with official cults aimed at preserving the state's stability. Although practices of popular religion left less evidence than official cults, they were an integral part of people's everyday lives, with the available evidence primarily based on the wealthier portion of the Egyptian population.

These practices included ceremonies related to significant life transitions such as birth, naming, and, especially, death, as they were believed to ensure the soul's survival in the afterlife. Other practices sought to discern the gods' will through dream interpretation and oracle consultation. People also performed magical rituals to influence the behavior of the gods for their benefit.

Individuals also engaged in acts of personal piety, praying to the gods and offering private offerings. Although evidence of this practice is scarce before the New Kingdom due to cultural restrictions on representing non-royal religious activities, it became more prominent as these restrictions relaxed. Official temples were important places for prayers and private offerings, and the population also used more accessible local chapels and shrines in their homes to worship gods or remember deceased family members.

At many Egyptian sacred sites, people worshiped individual animals believed to be manifestations of certain deities. These animals were selected based on specific markings believed to indicate their suitability for the role. Some, like the Apis bull worshiped in Memphis as a manifestation of Ptah, maintained their positions of worship throughout their lives, while others were selected for shorter periods. Over time, the popularity of these cults grew, and many temples began breeding animals to choose new divine manifestations. In the 26th Dynasty, a separate practice emerged where people mummified members of certain species as an offering to the gods these species represented, burying them in cemeteries near worship centers.

Magic:

In the popular religious practices of ancient Egypt, the deities invoked in everyday situations differed somewhat from those in state cult centers. Deities like the fertility goddess Taweret and the household protector Bes, although important to the population, did not have their own temples. However, other deities like Amun and Osiris were significant to both popular and official religion.

Some individuals showed devotion to a single god, often favoring those affiliated with their region or occupation. An example is the god Ptah, who, although especially important in his cult center in Memphis, received national veneration as the patron of artisans.

Regarding "magic" (heka in Egyptian terms), it was understood as the ability to make things happen through indirect means. Heka was believed to be a natural force used by the gods to create the universe and exert their will. Humans could also employ it, and magical practices were closely linked to religion. Even regular rituals performed in temples were considered forms of magic. Although some magical practices could have personal purposes, no form of magic was inherently considered hostile. Instead, it was mainly seen as a way to prevent or overcome negative events.

Magic in ancient Egypt was closely associated with priesthood, as temple libraries contained numerous magical texts. Reader priests, responsible for studying these texts, possessed extensive magical knowledge and often offered their services to common people. Other professions, such as doctors, scorpion charmers, and makers of magical amulets, also incorporated magical practices into their work. It is likely that even peasants used simple magic for their own purposes, although evidence of this is limited due to the oral transmission of such knowledge.

Language was intrinsically linked to magic, to the point where Thoth, the god of writing, was said to be the inventor of heka. Therefore, magic often involved written or spoken incantations, usually accompanied by ritual actions. These rituals often invoked the power of an appropriate deity to carry out the desired action, using heka to prompt the deity to act. In some cases, this involved the practitioner or the ritual's subject adopting the role of a mythological character, thus persuading the god to act in their favor. Additionally, rituals also made use of sympathetic magic, using objects believed to possess a significant magical resemblance to the ritual's subject. Objects considered imbued with heka, such as magical amulets used extensively by common Egyptians, were also employed.

Egyptians also used oracles to seek knowledge and guidance from the gods. These oracles are primarily known from the New Kingdom and later periods and were consulted to settle legal disputes or inform royal decisions. Common methods included asking questions of the divine image during festival processions and interpreting answers through the movement of the boat. Other methods involved observing the behavior of cult animals, casting lots, or consulting statues through which priests apparently spoke. Discerning the gods' will granted significant influence to priests interpreting their messages.

Funerary Practices:

Egyptian funerary practices were centered around the preservation of the body, considered essential for the survival of the soul. Initially, Egyptians buried their dead in the desert, where arid conditions naturally mummified the bodies. However, in the Early Dynastic Period, they began using tombs for greater protection. They developed elaborate embalming practices, where the corpse was artificially desiccated and wrapped to be placed in its coffin. The quality of the process varied based on cost, and those who couldn't afford it were buried in desert graves.

After the mummification process, the mummy was carried in a funeral procession from the deceased's home to the tomb, accompanied by friends, family, and various priests. Before burial, these priests performed rituals, such as the Opening of the Mouth ceremony, intended to restore the senses of the deceased and enable them to receive offerings. Subsequently, the mummy was buried, and the tomb was sealed. Later, relatives or priests offered food to the deceased in a nearby mortuary chapel at regular intervals. As time passed, families abandoned this practice for long-deceased relatives, and mortuary cults generally lasted only one or two generations. Nevertheless, while the cult was ongoing, the living sometimes wrote letters seeking help from deceased family members, believing that the dead could influence the world of the living similarly to the gods.

The early tombs in Egypt were known as mastabas, rectangular constructions made of bricks, intended to house kings and nobles in their final rest. These structures comprised an underground burial chamber and, at ground level, a chapel dedicated to funerary rituals. With the rise of the Old Kingdom, mastabas evolved into the iconic pyramids, symbolizing the primordial mound in Egyptian mythology. Reserved exclusively for royalty, these pyramids were accompanied by majestic mortuary temples at their bases. Although pharaohs of the Middle Kingdom continued to erect pyramids, the preference for mastabas decreased. Notably, common citizens with sufficient resources opted for rock-cut tombs, equipped with nearby mortuary chapels, a less tomb-robbery-prone choice. Even in the early stages of the New Kingdom, pharaohs adopted these rock-cut tombs, which were used until the decline of the religion itself.

These resting places not only housed bodies but also contained various objects, such as statues of the deceased serving as substitutes in case of body damage. Given the belief that the deceased should continue working in the afterlife, burials often included small models of individuals performing tasks, thus reflecting earthly life. Tombs of the economically prosperous could also contain household items, clothing, and other everyday objects intended for use in the afterlife. Amulets and magical objects provided additional protection against the dangers of the spiritual realm. Funerary texts, included in the burial, offered guidance and security in the afterlife. Tomb murals, adorned with art depicting the deceased enjoying food, were believed to magically enable them to receive sustenance even after mortuary offerings had ceased.

Languages:

Ancient Egyptian, in its various chronological stages, formed an independent part of the Afroasiatic (macro) family. Its closest relatives include groups like the Berbers, Semites, and Beja. Throughout Egyptian history, seven major divisions of the language are identified:

1. Archaic Egyptian (before 3000 BCE): Documented in inscriptions from the

late Predynastic and Archaic periods, with early evidence of hieroglyphic writing on Naqada II pottery.

2. Old Egyptian (3000-2000 BCE): The language of the Old Kingdom and the first intermediate period, characterized by the Pyramid Texts in aristocratic tombs.

3. Classical Egyptian (2000-1300 BCE): Also known as Middle Egyptian, it is marked by hieroglyphic and hieratic texts dating from the Middle Kingdom, covering funerary, medical, scientific, and poetic texts.

4. Late Egyptian (1300-700 BCE): Documents from this stage belong to the latter part of the New Kingdom, including religious and secular literature, such as the Story of Wenamun and the Instructions of Ani.

5. Demotic Egyptian (7th-4th centuries BCE): Used for economic and literary purposes, it became the dominant script around 600 BCE and was inscribed on stone and wood.

6. Egyptian Koine (3rd century BCE onwards): Following Alexander's conquest, the Koine dialect, a variant of Attic Greek used in the Hellenistic world, coexisted with Coptic used by the common people.

7. Coptic (3rd century CE onwards): As a spoken language from the 3rd to the 6th century, it persists only as the liturgical language of the Coptic Orthodox Church after being replaced by Arabic in the Islamic period. The Coptic name for Egypt is Ⲭⲏⲙⲓ (Kēmi).

Writing in Ancient Egypt:

Origins of Egyptian Writing:

The oldest known inscription was long believed to be the Narmer Palette, dated to 3150 BCE. However, recent findings in Gerzeh pottery, around 3250 BCE, reveal symbols resembling traditional hieroglyphs. In 1998, a German archaeological team discovered clay labels inscribed with hieroglyphs in the Umm el-Qaab necropolis in Abydos, dating to the Naqada III-a period, around 3300 BCE.

Development of Writing:

Egyptian writing is believed to have emerged around 3000 BCE, with the unification of the Upper and Lower Egypt. Initially, it consisted of around a thousand signs, hieroglyphs, representing various stylized forms of people, animals, plants, and objects. Over time, their number increased to several thousand in the Late Period.

Hieroglyphs and Cursive Forms:

Egyptian writing is considered the oldest in the world and is called "hieroglyphic," deriving from the Greek for "sacred" and "carve, engrave." It was partly syllabic and partly ideographic. The cursive form of hieroglyphs, known as hieratic, was used from the First Dynasty (c. 2925-2775 BCE). The demotic variant, both script and language, evolved during the Late Period.

Evolution of Writing:

Around 2700 BCE, pictograms began to represent consonant sounds, and by 2000 BCE, 26 were used to represent the 24 principal consonant sounds. The oldest known alphabet, an abjad system derived from these uniliteral signs, dates to around 1800 BCE.

Decline of Hieroglyphs:

Hieroglyphic writing ceased to be the main script around the 4th century BCE, under the Ptolemies, being replaced by Greek, although it persisted in the temples of Upper Egypt, guarded by the Egyptian clergy. Cleopatra VII was the only Ptolemaic ruler who mastered Ancient Egyptian. Its decipherment by Europeans began in the 15th century, although there were earlier attempts.

Literature:

The rich literary tradition of Egypt has its roots in Ancient Egypt, marking one of the earliest known literary expressions in human history. Egyptians were pioneers in developing a form of literature that has endured to this day.

Ancient Egyptian literature was recorded on papyri as well as on the surfaces of walls, tombs, pyramids, and obelisks. One notable example from this era is the "Tale of Sinuhe." Other notable texts include the "Westcar Papyrus," a collection of stories, and the "Ebers Papyrus," a pharmacopoeia treatise. Additionally, the "Book of the Dead," containing ritual instructions for the transition to the afterlife, reaches its most complete version in the well-known "Papyrus of Ani."

Ancient Egyptian literature is divided into religious and secular categories. Most of it is of a religious nature, addressing topics such as spells, funerary prayers, descriptions of the afterlife, and mythological narratives about the Ennead. In addition to the "Book of the Dead," the "Pyramid Texts," and the "Coffin Texts," inscriptions found in the tombs of the Valley of the Kings detailing the underworld are notable. Among these works are the "Book of Amduat," the "Book of Gates," the "Book of the Sacred Cow," the "Book of the Caverns," the "Book of the Earth," the "Book of Day and Night," and the "Litanies of Ra."

Secular literature in Egypt mainly encompasses wisdom books, intended for education rather than entertainment. A specific didactic sub-genre known as sebayt, which, to a certain extent, resembles the instruction of princes in the Christian tradition or adab in Muslim culture, was created. However, narratives, biographies, and love, elegiac, and philosophical poems were also produced for the purpose of entertaining, artistically expressing emotions, or reflecting on the meaning of life.

Autobiography:

Autobiography emerges as one of the oldest literary forms in Egypt, and examples have come down to us, such as those of Uni, the vizier, and that of Harkhuf. It is interesting to note the limited presence of the epic, with the "Poem of Pentaur" being the only preserved example that celebrates Ramses II's disputed victory at Qadesh.

Short Stories:

The short story was a highly valued genre, primarily transmitted orally. Its practice persisted into modern times, and Egypt made significant contributions to the tales found in "One Thousand and One Nights" in Arabic. Roger Lancelyn Green, an anthropologist and mythographer, compiled some stories that have reached us through inscriptions (such as "The Prince and the Sphinx" or "Ra and His Sons"), papyri ("The Golden Lotus" and "The Taking of Joppa"), or summaries transmitted by Greek writers like Stesichorus ("The Greek Princess") or Herodotus ("The Girl with the Red Shoes"), the latter being the oldest known version of the traditional Cinderella story.

Magical Texts:

Ritual and magical texts in ancient Egyptian civilization were written procedures on papyrus that served as instructions for those conducting religious rituals. These texts were primarily kept in temple libraries and were often inscribed in the temples themselves, sometimes accompanied by illustrations. Unlike ritual papyri, temple inscriptions were not instructions but symbolically perpetuated rituals, even if they ceased to be practiced in reality.

Additionally, magical texts were developed, describing rituals, but their purpose was to achieve specific goals in daily life. Although they had worldly objectives, many of these texts originated in temples and over time spread among the general population.

In terms of hymns and prayers, the Egyptians created numerous hymns and prayers in the form of poetry, written on papyrus and on the walls of temples. Hymns were intended to praise specific deities and were recited as part of rituals in temples. They were structured according to literary formulas that presented the mythological nature and functions of a deity. Prayers, on the other hand, followed the pattern of hymns but addressed the god more personally, seeking blessings, help, or forgiveness for misdeeds. These prayers were rare before the New Kingdom, indicating that direct and personal interaction with a deity was not considered possible in the early periods or at least was less likely to be expressed in writing. These prayers are primarily known for being inscribed on statues and stelae left in sacred places as votive offerings.

Funerary Texts:

Among the most significant and extensively preserved Egyptian writings are funerary texts, designed to ensure that the souls of the deceased reach a pleasant afterlife. The earliest of these is the Pyramid Texts, a collection of hundreds of spells inscribed on the walls of royal pyramids during the Old Kingdom. These spells were magically intended to provide pharaohs with the means to join the company of the gods in the afterlife and appeared in different arrangements and combinations, some present throughout the entire pyramid.

At the end of the Old Kingdom, a new set of funerary spells emerged, including material from the Pyramid Texts. These were mainly inscribed on coffins and were known as the Coffin Texts. Unlike the Pyramid Texts, they were not reserved exclusively for royalty but appeared in non-royal officials' tombs. In the New Kingdom, several additional funerary texts were developed, with the most well-known being the Book of the Dead. Unlike earlier books, this often contained extensive illustrations or vignettes. The book was copied onto papyrus and sold to commoners to be placed in their tombs.

The Coffin Texts included sections with detailed descriptions of the underworld and instructions on how to overcome its dangers. In the New Kingdom, this material gave rise to various "books of the underworld," such as the Book of the Gates, the Book of the Caverns, and the Amduat. Unlike loose collections of spells, these books of the underworld were structured representations of Ra's journey through the Duat and, by analogy, the deceased person's soul journey through the realm of the dead. Initially restricted to pharaonic tombs, their use expanded in the Third Intermediate Period.

With the advancement and modernization of Egypt, ancient practices were replaced by new and efficient scientific techniques, including improvements in mummification, allowing the Egyptians to achieve a new level of excellence in their preparation for the afterlife.

Religion in Ancient Egypt:

Religion in Ancient Egypt was a central component of Egyptian life, permeating all aspects from the predynastic period to the arrival of Christianity and Islam during the Greco-Roman and Arab periods. Here are some key points about Egyptian religion:

1. Mythology and Priests:

   - Egyptian religion was embodied in mythology and led by priests. Priests played a crucial role in administering religious practices and rituals.

2. Sacred Temples:

   - Temples were sacred places restricted to priests and priestesses, although on special occasions, the people were admitted to the temple courtyard during important celebrations.

3. Transmission of Beliefs:

   - The presence of mummies and pyramids outside of Egypt suggests that the beliefs and values of Egyptian culture were transmitted through trade routes. Contacts with various regions such as Nubia, Punt, the Aegean, Greece, Lebanon, and Libya influenced Egyptian beliefs.

4. Influence on the Arts:

- The religious nature of Egyptian civilization influenced its artistic contributions. Many works depict gods, goddesses, and pharaohs considered divine. Egyptian art is characterized by symmetry and order.

5. Animals in Religion:

- Throughout the 3000 years of independent culture, animals portrayed or worshipped in art, writing, and religion were indigenous to Africa. Although the dromedary, of Arabian origin, appeared in Egypt in the 2nd millennium BCE.

6. Health Issues Related to Practices:

- Analysis of mummies has revealed evidence of a stable diet during the Middle Kingdom. However, older mummies show signs of anemia and hemolytic disorders, suggesting poisoning by heavy metals used in pigments, dyes, and makeup.

Egyptian religion was a unifying force in society and left a lasting impact on the culture and artistic practices of Ancient Egypt. The essence of religion in Ancient Egypt was woven as a complex system of beliefs that penetrated deeply into ancestral Egyptian society. At its core, it focused on the interaction of Egyptians with various deities, considered controllers of natural forces and elements. Religious practices were acts intended to provide for the gods and gain their favor. The pharaoh, as the king of Egypt, played a central role, being seen as the incarnation of Horus, invested with divine power by his position. His responsibility was to sustain the gods through rituals and offerings, ensuring the maintenance of universal order. The state dedicated considerable resources to these rituals and temple construction.

On an individual level, Egyptians interacted with the gods for their own purposes, either through prayers or through the use of black magic. Although distinct, these practices were closely related to formal rituals and institutions. As the pharaoh's status declined throughout Egyptian history, popular religious tradition gained prominence. Additionally, belief in the afterlife and funerary practices were fundamental aspects. Egyptians made great efforts to ensure the survival of the soul after death, providing tombs, burial goods, and offerings to preserve the bodies and spirits of the deceased.

Rooted in Egyptian prehistory, religion endured for more than 3000 years, permeating every aspect of Egyptian culture. It is notable that the Egyptian language lacked a term equivalent to the modern European concept of religion. The religion of Ancient Egypt did not adopt a monolithic structure; rather, it consisted of an extensive and diverse set of beliefs and practices, united by their shared focus on the interaction between the human and divine worlds. The characteristics of the gods inhabiting the divine realm were intrinsically linked to the Egyptian understanding of the properties of the world they lived in.

Egyptians conceived natural phenomena as intrinsic divine forces. These deified forces encompassed elements, animal attributes, and abstract forces. They believed in a pantheon of gods involved in all aspects of nature and human society. Religious practices sought to maintain and appease these phenomena to make them favorable to humans. This polytheistic system was complex, as some deities were believed to exist in different manifestations and had multiple mythological roles. In turn, many natural forces, such as the sun, were associated with multiple deities. The diversity of the pantheon ranged from gods with vital functions in the universe to minor or local deities. It even included gods adopted from foreign cultures and, at times, human beings, such as deceased pharaohs, who were considered divine, and prominent individuals like Imhotep, who were also deified.

Artistic representations of the gods were not intended to be literal interpretations of their appearance in case they were real. The true nature of the gods was believed to be mysterious. Instead, these representations granted recognizable forms to abstract deities through symbolic images that indicated each god's role in nature. For example,

Anubis, the funerary god, was depicted as a jackal, a creature whose scavenging habits threatened the preservation of the body, but this threat was reversed for protection. Anubis's black skin symbolized the color of mummified flesh and the fertile black soil associated with resurrection. This iconography was not static, and many gods could be represented in various forms.

Several gods were linked to specific regions of Egypt, where their cults were prominent. However, these associations varied over time, and a god's connection to a place did not necessarily imply that their cult originated there. For instance, the god Monthu was the initial patron of the city of Thebes, but during the Middle Kingdom, Amun displaced him in that role, likely emerging from another location. The popularity and national importance of individual gods fluctuated similarly over time.

Egyptian gods maintained complex interrelationships that partly reflected the interaction of the forces they represented. Egyptians often grouped gods to illustrate these relationships, either in groups of indeterminate size related by similar functions or in combinations based on the symbolic significance of numbers in Egyptian mythology, representing the duality of opposing phenomena.

One of the most common combinations was the family triad, consisting of a father, a mother, and a child, worshipped together. Another group of great importance was the Ennead, bringing together nine deities in a theological system that encompassed mythological areas of creation, reign, and life after death.

The relationships between deities were also expressed through syncretism, where two or more different gods were linked to form a composite deity. This process acknowledged the presence of one god "in" another, as the second god assumed a role that belonged to the first. These connections between deities were fluid and did not represent a permanent fusion, allowing some gods to develop multiple syncretic connections. Sometimes, syncretism united deities with similar characteristics, while at other times, it united gods of different natures, as in the case of Amun-Ra, combining hidden power with the great visible force of nature.

During the New Kingdom, Pharaoh Akhenaten took a radical step by abolishing the official worship of other gods in favor of the solar disk Aten. Although some interpret this as an early indication of true monotheism, Atenist theology remains unclear, and the idea that Akhenaten practiced monolatry instead of monotheism is disputed. Akhenaten did not actively deny the existence of other gods; he simply refrained from worshiping those who were not Aten. After his reign, Egypt returned to its traditional religion, and Akhenaten was denounced as a heretic.

Important Concepts

The central concept in the Egyptian worldview was "Ma'at," a word that encompassed several concepts in Spanish, including "truth," "justice," and "order." Ma'at represented the fixed and eternal order of the universe, both in the cosmos and in human society. It was essential for the cohesion of the world and existed since its creation. According to Egyptian belief, Ma'at was always threatened by forces of disorder, so the entire society had the responsibility to maintain it.

In the human realm, this involved the cooperation and coexistence of all members of society. On a cosmic level, it meant that all forces of nature, personified as gods, had to maintain balance. This goal was central to Egyptian religion, where Egyptians sought to sustain the gods through offerings and rituals to ward off disorder and perpetuate natural cycles.

The Egyptian conception of time in their worldview was deeply linked to Ma'at. Through the linear passage of time, Egyptians saw a cyclical pattern that renewed Ma'at through periodic events reflecting the original creation. Events such as the annual flooding of the Nile, the succession of kings, and the daily journey of the sun god Ra were crucial to maintaining cosmic order.

The Egyptian vision of the cosmos portrayed the earth as a flat expanse personified by the god Geb, with the sky goddess Nut arching over it, separated by the air god Shu. Beneath the earth existed parallel underworld and under-sky realms, and beyond the skies was the infinite expanse of Nu, the chaos that existed before creation. Additionally, Egyptians believed in a place called Duat, associated with death and rebirth.

In this cosmos, there were three types of sentient beings: gods, spirits of the deceased existing in the divine realm, and humans. The pharaoh held a special place as a bridge between the human and divine realms, being the most important among humans.

The divinity of the pharaoh in ancient Egyptian culture has been a topic of debate among Egyptologists. It is likely that Egyptians considered royal authority as a divine force, viewing the pharaoh not only as human but also as a god incarnate due to the divine power inherent in the monarchy. This duality allowed the pharaoh to play the crucial role of intermediary between the population and the gods, being fundamental to maintaining Ma'at in both human society and religious rituals.

Although they recognized the humanity and weaknesses of the pharaoh, the perception of his divinity was rooted in the belief that he personified the divine power of the state. As a result, the pharaoh oversaw all religious activities of the state and had the responsibility to uphold justice and harmony in society, as well as to sustain the gods through temples and offerings.

Despite this elevated position, the religious importance of the pharaoh significantly diminished towards the end of the New Kingdom, and the gap between his idealized role in official writings and representations and his influence in real life and prestige could be considerable.

The pharaoh was closely associated with various specific deities. He was directly identified with Horus, symbolizing monarchy, and considered the son of Ra, who ruled nature in analogy to how the pharaoh governed society. During the New Kingdom, he was also associated with Amun, the supreme force of the cosmos. After his death, the pharaoh attained a fully deified state, directly identified with Ra and associated with Osiris, the god of death and rebirth, and the mythical father of Horus. Numerous mortuary temples were dedicated to the worship of deceased pharaohs as divinities.

Life after Death in Ancient Egypt

The ancient Egyptians developed detailed beliefs about death and the afterlife. They held the idea that humans possessed a "ka," a life force that left the body upon death. In life, the ka consumed food and drink, so it was believed that, to endure after death, the ka must continue to receive spiritual offerings of food. Each individual also had a "ba," comprising the unique spiritual characteristics of the person. Unlike the ka, the ba remained attached to the body after death. Egyptian funerary rituals aimed to release the ba from the body so that it could move freely and reunite with the ka, giving rise to the emergence of the "akh." Additionally, preserving the body was considered crucial, as the ba returned each night to receive new life before emerging in the morning as an akh.

Initially, it was believed that only the pharaoh had a ba, and only he could merge with the gods, while deceased commoners went to a dark and desolate realm opposed to life. Nobles received tombs and resources for their maintenance as gifts from the king, and their access to the afterlife depended on these royal favors. In the early times, it was thought that deceased pharaohs ascended to the sky and dwelled among the stars. However, during the Old Kingdom, the pharaoh's figure became closely associated with the daily rebirth of the sun god Ra and the ruler of the underworld Osiris, as the importance of these deities grew.

By the end of the Old Kingdom (2686-2181 BCE) and the First Intermediate Period (c. 2181-2055 BCE), Egyptians began to gradually develop the belief that possession of a "ba" and the opportunity to experience a paradisiacal afterlife extended to everyone. In the more elaborate beliefs about the afterlife during the New Kingdom, it was asserted that the soul had to face various supernatural dangers in the Duat before undergoing a final judgment known as the "Weighing of the Heart." In this judgment, the gods evaluated the actions of the deceased while alive (symbolized by the heart) compared to the Ma'at, determining whether the individual had behaved in accordance with this fundamental principle. It was commonly said that the deceased inhabited the realm of Osiris, a prosperous and pleasant land in the underworld.

The solar vision of the afterlife, in which the souls of the deceased traveled with Ra on his daily journey, remained primarily associated with royalty but extended to others as well. Throughout the Middle and New Kingdoms, the idea that the "akh" could travel in the world of the living and, to some extent, magically influence events in this world, became increasingly common.

Belief in an afterlife was fundamental in the religion and culture of Ancient Egypt. Key aspects of this belief include:

1. Preparation for the Future Life:

Egyptians prepared for the afterlife by following established norms, such as those found in the "Book of the Dead." They also dedicated efforts to prepare both the tomb and the deceased's body to ensure a successful transition to the afterlife.

2. Division of the Ka:

They believed that after death, the ka (double in spirit form) split into ba (soul) and akh (spirit). The ba resided in the deceased's tomb and had the freedom to move. The akh headed to the underworld to face judgment.

3. Judgment in the Underworld:

Osiris, the great god of the underworld, presided over the judgment of the akh. Anubis weighed the deceased's heart on a scale, while Ma'at, the goddess of truth and justice, placed her feather on the other side. If the heart was as light as the feather, the spirit joined good spirits in a life of peace and harmony. Otherwise, it faced eternal punishments.

4. Construction of Tombs and Pyramids:

Building tombs and pyramids was essential to provide a home for the ba and akh in the afterlife. Objects, jewelry, clothes, food, and games were left in the tomb for the deceased's use in their other life.

5. Fear of Tomb Robbery:

Egyptians feared tomb robbery, as it could leave the ba homeless and result in a more severe second death. Sometimes, statues of the deceased were placed in pyramids as an alternative to provide shelter for the ba.

6. Participation in the Future Life:

Initially, only pharaohs had the right to participate in the afterlife. However, over time, this belief extended to all Egyptians, and each individual strove to prepare their tomb and body according to their economic means.

The afterlife held a central place in the Egyptian conception of the cosmos, and practices associated with it were essential in the society and religion of Ancient Egypt.

Egyptian Mythology:

Egyptian mythology, practiced for over three thousand years, was the fundamental basis for the organization of society in Ancient Egypt. However, in 535 AD, during the reign of Justinian I and with the rise of Christianity, its practice was prohibited. This belief influenced all aspects of life, from the power structure with the pharaoh to funeral practices.

Among the major gods of Egyptian mythology are Ra, Amun, Anubis, Aten, Horus, Osiris, Hapi, Atum, Bes, Ptah, Seth, Thoth, Apis, Bastet, Hathor, Isis, Maat, Nephthys, and Tefnut.

Initially, the religion of the Egyptians was polytheistic, with many gods from diverse origins and no clear classification. Egyptians seemed to take particular pleasure in multiplying their gods through various imaginative and circumstantial means.

During this chaotic time, Amon-Ra, the great Being, the Eternal, was worshipped, with his companion receiving different names depending on the locations, such as Neith, Muth, or Buto. Knufis or Knet was the creative spirit of the Universe, the great demiurge. Ptah was considered the great organizer and preserver. Menoes was equivalent to the Hellenic Pan, Suk to Cronus,

Dyom to Janus or Jupiter, Thme to Justice, Thoth to Hermes, Hathor to Venus, and Anuké to Vasta.

To add to the confusion, each of these gods was worshipped in different forms, sometimes with a human form, a human body and the head of the animal it symbolized, or under the figure of that same animal.

To bring some clarity and order to Egyptian mythology, it is useful to divide their gods into three classes:

- **Primordial Gods and their Derivatives.**

- **Sideral and Physical Gods.**

- **Gods with Human and Historical Forms.**

Sideral Gods in Egypt:

Immediately after these three gods, but before the remaining deities, were the twelve sideral gods, the six male Cabiros and the six female Cabiros, each of whom had a sphere or space to govern. They were believed to be children of Ftha and were ruled by Fre.

The male Cabiros were named: Djom, Pi, Ertosi, Surot, Pi-Hermón, and Remfa.

The female Cabiros: Illit (the moon), Saté (the ether), Anuké (fire), Buto (the atmosphere), Hathor (water), and Nephthys (earth).

Following the Cabiros were the Decans, lower deities, each of whom had influence over a third of the zodiac sign, numbering thirty-six in total.

The twelve Cabiros are represented presiding over specific zodiac signs, and beneath each Cabiro, there is a group of three Decans. The Decans were the tutelary geniuses of the horoscope, and each was attributed a certain power, both for good and for ill. The tutelary genius of each person was the Decan-Horoscope that governed at their birth.

Primordial God in Egypt:

The primordial god was called Piromi, the sublime; this god existed from eternity in an inactive state. When it decided to create, it was called Knef. Piromi, the creator of light or transformed into light, was referred to as Ftha. Piromi Sun was given the name Fre.

These three gods, Knef, Ftha, Fre—essentially one and the same—formed the first Egyptian trinity. Each of them is Piromi. Together, the three are Piromi. Knef, the creator, both male and female simultaneously, united with the divine word, and from this union was born the second demiurge Ftha, the god of fire and life, who, in turn, created Earth (Tho) and the sky (Potiris). As both male and female, Ftha split and gave rise to

Pan-Mendes, the male power of production, and Hefestobula, the female power of generation.

From the divine coupling emerged Pi-Re or Fre, the Sun, and Pi-Ioh, the Moon; the former, the right eye of the sky, and the latter, the left eye.

Therefore, the eight main deities of primitive Egypt were: Piromi - Buto, Knef - Neith, Ftha - Athor, and Fre-Athor; eternal deities, emanations, or transformations of the supreme intelligence.

Knef, the first revelation of Piromi and the first deity of the supreme triad (Knef, Ptha, and Fre), was known by numerous names: Nef, Nev Nub, Nuf, Num, all without the initial K.

Joined with the different attributes assigned to the same god in each locality, it led to the belief that they were different gods rather than one and the same. Thus, Ammon was the very Knef; and since the priests knew that the three gods of the triad were one god, they gave the name of Ammon to each of them: Ammon-Knef, Ammon-Ftha, and Ammon-Fre. From then on, Ammon summed up all the names of the most sublime god for the Egyptians. The most magnificent temples in the entire country were dedicated to Ammon.

Ftha, the second person of the Egyptian trinity, was also the second manifestation of the primordial god, Piromi; possibly believed to be the son of Knef and Neith. In a succession order,

Piromi is the preexisting god; Knef, the creative will, and Ftha, the primal fire.

From Ftha, organizer and craftsman of the world, came two deities: Ftha, male, or Pan-Mendes, and Ftha, female, or Athor, the golden Venus.

Something similar to what happened with Ammon occurred with Ftha-Athor. It was confused with Neith, with Buto, and was later individualized as Isis-Athor. And already with this name or with the name Isis, it assumed the representation of the feminine element of divinity.

Fre, also called Ra, is the third demiurge or the third manifestation of the incommunicable Piromi. In the theological and transcendental language of Egypt, Fre is the one emanating from Ftha. Fre is the individualized fire, the light-fire, the Sun. From Fre emanated: the planets, the suns —of each day, the rising and setting, of each season of the year—earthly gods whose adventures reflect celestial phenomena, various heroic personifications.

Being the only one of the great gods visible, Fre was considered the great god, and some mythologists even placed him at the head of the first triad.

Incarnations in Egyptian Mythology

In Egyptian theology, the system of incarnations was of paramount importance, leading to the worship of animals believed to embody the gods. Osiris incarnated in the black bull Apis, distinguished by a triangular white spot on the forehead, another on the right side in the shape of a crescent, and one on the back. Osiris-Apis is depicted with the solar disk between its horns.

Sejet was the cat goddess, the daughter of the Sun, and a punisher of wrongdoers in the underworld. Thot incarnated in the ibis, a herald of the Nile floods and a symbol of wisdom. Typhon incarnated in the hippopotamus.

Various animals were revered in different regions: the weasel in Thebes, the shrew in Buto, the he-goat in Mendes, the goat in Coptos, and the kite in Hierakonpolis.

Cult of Serapis:

Nevertheless, during the Ptolemaic dynasty, all Egyptian divinities took a back seat with the emergence of the cult of Serapis. This god, considered equivalent to Osiris-Apis or, more accurately, to the deceased Apis worshipped in Memphis and a small chapel erected along the coastal rocks.

Serapis accumulated all the divine attributes, receiving all honors combined. Serapis became assimilated with Ammon, Knef, Zeus, and Apollo, as the Egyptians sought to identify their deities with those of the Greeks. Serapis formed a triad with Isis and Horus. The cult of Serapis spread across Asia, Thrace, Greece, and Italy, boasting forty-three magnificent temples in Egypt alone, according to the orator Aristides in the 2nd century CE.

Serapis's main attributes included the cylindrical tiara, lotus flowers, zodiac signs, and a spiral serpent around its horn. Its visage bore a striking resemblance to that of Olympian Zeus.

Sources of Egyptian Myth:

Few narratives from Egyptian civilization have survived, leading to the reconstruction of myths from indirect sources. Religious texts, funerary rituals, hymns, and magical texts contribute to understanding Egyptian myths. Pictorial representations in tombs, temples, and pyramids provide additional insights, primarily from 1500 BCE or later.

Major Egyptian myths may also appear in literary texts in a different format.

Local Myths:

Many deities were regionally significant or featured in local variations of national gods. Some myths explained local features like the origin of a mountain or associations with an ancient building. Others, particularly well-known during the Greco-Roman period, gained prominence nationwide.

Chronology of the Egyptian Civilization:

Period	Dates (BCE)	Notes
Predynastic	6000 - 3150	Development of early settlements
Early Dynastic	3150 - 2686	Unification of Upper and Lower Egypt
Old Kingdom	2686 - 2181	Construction of pyramids
First Intermediate	2181 - 2055	Political decentralization
Middle Kingdom	2055 - 1650	Reunification and cultural flourishing
Second Intermediate	1650 - 1550	Hyksos invasion and foreign rule
New Kingdom	1550 - 1070	Expansion, military and conquests
Third Intermediate	1070 - 664	Decline in centralized power
Late Period	664 - 332	Persian and Greek influence

Period	Dates (BCE)	Notes
Ptolemaic Period	332 - 30	Rule by the Ptolemaic dynasty
Roman Period	30 BCE - 395 CE	Annexation by the Roman Empire
Byzantine Period	395 - 641	Rule under the Eastern Roman Empire
Arab Period	641 onwards	Arab-Muslim conquest and cultural change

Thebes

Thebes, the present-day Luxor, served as the capital from around 2000 BCE to approximately 1520-1450 BCE. It was the primary religious center for over a millennium and is the site with the largest temple complexes in the ancient world, along with the royal burials of the Valley of the Kings. Its main deity, Amun, perhaps originated in another region and replaced the falcon god Montu of Armant.

Creation

Despite the lack of unified religious scriptures, the Egyptians produced numerous religious texts of various kinds. These diverse texts, when combined, offer an extensive yet still incomplete understanding of Egyptian religious practices and beliefs.

As for Egyptian myths, they were metaphorical narratives intended to illustrate and explain the actions and roles of the gods in nature. The details of these events could change to convey different symbolic perspectives of the mysterious divine events they described, leading to the existence of various, and sometimes conflicting, versions of the myths. The lack of fully written mythic narratives and the presence of scattered episodes or allusions in the texts mean that knowledge of Egyptian mythology is primarily derived from hymns, ritual and magical texts, as well as funerary texts mentioning the roles of deities in the afterlife. Additionally, some myths were recorded by Greeks and Romans, such as Plutarch, towards the end of Egyptian history.

Among the significant Egyptian myths are creation myths that narrate the emergence of the world from the primordial ocean of chaos. These stories describe the creation process in various ways, such as the transformation of the primordial god Atum, the creative speech of the intellectual god Ptah, and the act of the hidden power of Amun. Despite these variations, the act of creation represents the initial establishment of Ma'at and sets the pattern for subsequent cycles of time.

The most important myth in Egyptian mythology is the Osiris and Isis myth. This tale recounts the story of Osiris, a divine ruler murdered by his jealous brother Seth, associated with chaos. Isis, Osiris's wife, resurrected him to conceive their heir, Horus. Osiris became the ruler of the dead in the underworld, and Horus, upon growing up, defeated Seth to become king. Seth's association with chaos provided a foundation for pharaonic succession, portraying pharaohs as maintainers of order. This myth is also linked to the Egyptian agricultural cycle and serves as a model for the resurrection of human souls.

Another significant mythical motif is Ra's nightly journey through the Duat. During this journey, Ra encounters Osiris, acting as a regeneration agent, renewing Ra's life. Additionally, Ra faces Apophis, a serpent god of chaos, each night. The defeat of Apophis and the reunion with Osiris ensure the sun's ascent at dawn, symbolizing rebirth and the triumph of order over chaos.

While Christian theology has a single creation narrative, ancient Egypt has recorded four stories. Each creation story is associated with a significant city:

- Heliopolis,

- Memphis,

- Hermopolis, and

- Esna,

as well as a fundamental god: Atum—later equated with Ra—Ptah, Thoth, and Khnum, respectively.

Creation: Benu Bird

The Benu bird is also related to the solar cult of Heliopolis. In Egyptian art, it was depicted as a royal heron, but there are references to it as a phoenix, a symbol of resurrection (in other mythologies, it rises from the ashes of its own funeral pyre). In a papyrus from the 13th century BCE, the Benu bird, venerated in Heliopolis as the first deity, was identified by the Greeks with the phoenix, which burns every fifty years and is reborn from its ashes.

In Heliopolis, the Benu bird is depicted perching on the tip of a small pyramid-shaped stone, the benben. This gave rise to the impressive pairs of obelisks that stood before the towering protective pylons at the entrance of temples. Devoted to the solar god, their pyramidical tips were often adorned with gold, silver, or electrum (a natural alloy of gold and silver) so that they could capture and reflect the first rays of the sun, the god Ra-Horakhty, "rising on his horizon." Many of these obelisks disappeared from Egypt since the end of ancient times and now adorn some modern capitals, where they are mistakenly called "Cleopatra's Needles," despite being much older and having nothing to do with the last Egyptian pharaoh, who ended her life in August of the year 30 B.C.

Creation: Esna

In Esna, the temple was dedicated to the ram-headed god Khnum. It was believed that he had formed humans on his potter's wheel, though in duplicate, as each person had a ka, a double. This was the spirit that remained near the deceased's tomb, while their ba, their soul, in the form of a bird with a human head, would fly to the other world upon death. The most complete version of creation is carved on the walls of the Esna temple and tells of a goddess named Neith, associated with the city of Sais in the Delta, who emerged even before the primordial mound rose from the Waters of Nun to create the world.

While for a modern religious mind, four basic versions of the creation story might be a source of unease and uncertainty, ancient Egyptians had no problem with it. Each legend about creation had its place, although the Heliopolis version held a prominent position due to its connection with the sun and the chief of the gods, Ra, who later assimilated with Thebes' Amun to become the great god Amun-Ra.

Creation: Heliopolis

In Heliopolis, the City of the Sun, Atum stood alone on a dune that had emerged from the primordial Waters of Nun, which covered the world (similar to the flooding of the Nile). Realizing the need for other gods to assist in creation, Atum masturbated, and from his semen emerged two other gods: Shu, the god of the sky, and Tefnut, his sister, the goddess of moisture. Their children were Geb, the god of the earth, and Nut, the goddess of the sky (such relationships, consanguineous marriages, usually deemed incestuous in the modern world, were not uncommon in ancient mythology). In the papyri, Nut is depicted arched over Geb, with Shu separating them into their respective spheres. Geb and Nut had five children: Osiris, Isis, Horus the Elder, Set, and Nephthys—born on five consecutive days, outside the normal 360-day calendar.

This occurred (reflected in classical mythology) due to a prophecy that the children of Nut would surpass Atum-Ra in power (similar to the children of Cronus, through Rhea, overthrowing their father). By being born on days not in the calendar, the curse that Nut would not give birth on any day of the year was resolved.

Creation: Memphis and Hermopolis

Memphis

In Memphis, the traditional capital of Egypt since the First Dynasty (circa 3100 B.C.), the principal deity was the creator god Ptah. According to legend, Ptah preceded Atum, as he formed the heart and tongue of the latter. Ptah was especially revered as the god of craftsmen and manual workers, and among his many titles was "father and mother of all the gods."

Hermopolis

A third creation legend was found in Hermopolis, a revered center of worship for the god Thoth. He was often depicted with the head of an ibis, and the baboon was a sacred animal associated with him. Thoth was the god of wisdom and study, as well as the inventor of hieroglyphics, a term that literally meant "sacred writings." He was particularly the patron god of scribes and also had a connection with the moon.

A variant around the creation legend states that it was in Hermopolis, not Heliopolis, where the primordial mound emerged from the Waters of Nun. From an egg resting on the mound, the sun god emerged. In another alternative version, it is said that a lotus flower grew on the mound, and its leaves opened to reveal the young god of creation, Nefertum.

The Origin of the World in Egypt

The Arrangement that Arises from Chaos

Before the appearance of gods in Egypt, there existed only a dark watery abyss, the Nun, whose chaotic energies contained the potential form of all living beings. The spirit of the creator was present in these primordial waters, but there was no place for it to come to life. The great serpent Apep or Apophis embodied the destructive forces of chaos.

The event that marked the beginning of time was the emergence of the first land, rising from the waters of the Nun and providing a foundation for the first deity. In some cases, it took the form of a bird or a heron, perched on the mound of primordial land. According to another version of creation, the primordial lotus emerges from the waters and, upon opening, reveals a divine child.

The first deity was endowed with various divine powers, such as Hu ("Authoritative Word"), Sia ("Perception"), and Heka ("Magic"). Using these powers, it transformed chaos into order, divine order personified by the goddess Maat, daughter of the sun god. The term Maat also means justice, truth, and harmony.

Divine order was constantly at risk of dissolving into the chaos from which it had originated.

The first deity became aware of its solitude and created gods and humans in its image and likeness, along with a world for them to inhabit. According to the myth, gods originated from the sweat of the sun god, and humans from its tears.

Generally, creative power is linked to the sun, but there are various deities considered creators. In the temple of the sun god in Heliopolis, the Benu bird was the first deity. Represented as a heron, the radiant bird was a manifestation of the sun's creator god, bringing light to the darkness of chaos. When it landed on the primordial land, it emitted a cry, the first sound.

Destruction

After the creation of the world and humanity, gods proliferated; many of them were closely related, much like the 12 gods of Olympus in Greek mythology. And, just as in the Christian tradition, there is a tale of destruction.

Humans were too preoccupied with themselves and were forgetting the gods, failing to present them with due offerings. Ra, the chief of the gods, consulted with the others to determine how to punish humans and compel them to continue religious observances.

They agreed to send Sejmet, a lion-headed goddess representing the vigor of the midday sun and thus the personification of evil capable of killing humans, to the earth. There, she embarked on an indiscriminate killing spree, delighting in the taste of blood.

The gods were horrified to discover the final outcome, the extinction of humanity, but Sejmet displayed a genuine bloodthirsty lust seemingly without end.

Finally, the gods managed to thwart her plans through deception: they flooded a field with a red potion (jakadi) that appeared as blood but was made from a mixture of strong beer.

Sejmet indulged in it and fell into a deep slumber. Upon waking, the slaughter had concluded, and humans had learned the lesson not to neglect the gods.

The Ogdoad

In ancient Egypt, the forces of chaos could be personified in eight deities, the Ogdoad.

The Ogdoad consisted of four pairs, each symbolizing an aspect of the primordial state.

Nun and Naunet were the god and goddess of primordial waters, Kek and Keket were deities of darkness, Amón and Amaunet embodied an invisible power, and Heh and Hehet represented the limitless.

Sometimes, additional pairs were included in the Ogdoad, but the total number of deities was always eight, imagined in the form of snakes and frogs, beings of primordial slime. In other instances, they appear as baboons celebrating the first birth of the sun.

The Egyptians primarily revered the Ogdoad in a place called Khemenu ("Eighth City"), and the Greeks in Hermopolis, the site of the "Island of Fire," where the sun was born for the first time.

The Ogdoad united to form the cosmic egg, in which the sun god was incubated. It is said that a portion of the shell of the cosmic egg is buried in the temple of Hermopolis.

Creator Gods

The Egyptians had four main creator deities: Amun-Ra, Aten, Khnum, and Ptah, each the focus of significant cults.

Amun-Ra: A member of the Ogdoad, worshipped as the god of fertility in Thebes, Upper Egypt. In the II millennium, he became the national god, merging his name with the supreme solar deity, Ra, resulting in Amun-Ra, the hidden power that empowered the gods. Amun, in the form of a serpent, was the first being from the primordial waters, fertilizing the cosmic egg formed by the other members of the Ogdoad. In another myth, Amun, in the form of a goose, laid the cosmic egg from which life emerged.

Aten: A creator deity worshipped in Heliopolis, emerging from primordial chaos in the form of a serpent but typically depicted in human form. As Aten-Ra, he represented the evening sun that had to return to the womb of Nut to renew every night. Like other creator deities, Aten represented a totality containing both masculine and feminine aspects. In an ancient myth, feeling lonely in the primordial land, Aten holds his phallus and produces semen, giving rise to the first divine couple, Shu and Tefnut.

The Hand of Aten

In a reinterpretation of the Aten myth, creation began with the sexual union of a god and a goddess. The feminine element is identified with the hand of Aten. Among the various goddesses called "the hand," the most significant were Hathor and Neith. This faience head combines the attributes of Hathor and Nut, another goddess embodying feminine creative power.

Khnum: The main center of Khnum's worship was on the southern island of Elephantine. He was believed to control the annual flooding of the Nile and embodied the life-giving power of the inundation. His sacred animal was the ram, a symbol of virility, and he was typically depicted as a man with the head of this animal. In his temple in Esna, he is described as the "father of fathers and mother of mothers," molding gods, people, and animals with clay on his potter's wheel and breathing life into them.

Ptah: Adored in Memphis, Ptah was the god of the arts, shaping gods and kings with precious metals. The intellectual force behind creation, he made other gods by thinking of them and speaking their names aloud.

The Ennead

In the Egyptian creation narrative that provides more details, the deities known as the nine gods of Heliopolis, the Ennead (from the Greek term ennea, meaning nine), take center stage.

The first is Aten-Ra, who came to life on the primordial mound of earth and conceived the multiplicity of creation in his heart. He made the first division between the masculine and the feminine by placing his semen in his mouth and spitting out Shu, the god of air, and Tefnut, the goddess of moisture. Both explored the dark Nun and got lost, but Aten-Ra sent his divine eye, a powerful force considered the daughter of the sun god, to search for them.

The goddess returned with Shu and Tefnut, and the first human beings emerged from the tears that Aten-Ra shed upon reuniting with his children.

From the sexual union of Shu and Tefnut, Geb, the god of earth, and Nut, the goddess of the sky, were born. They embraced so closely that there was no space for anything to exist between them. Geb impregnated Nut, but she couldn't give birth to her children until Shu, their father, separated them. With the help of eight beings known as Heh gods, Shu held the sky goddess above the earth, leaving enough space for living beings and the air they needed to breathe.

The Egyptians believed that another sky existed beneath the earth.

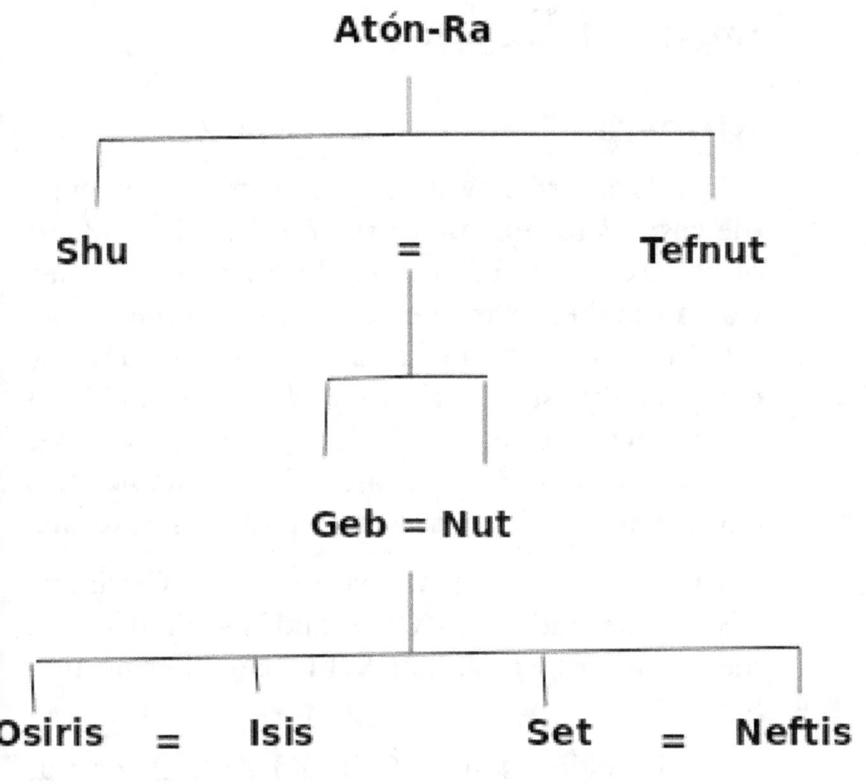

Family tree of the Ennead

Gods of Egypt

Atón-ra

The primordial waters continued to surround the cosmos formed by earth and sky. The goddess of the sky sometimes took the form of a naked woman arched over the earth and at other times that of a cow fashioned with stars. It was said that every night she swallowed the sun and was sometimes accused of wanting to devour her children as well. In these cases, Nut was depicted as a pig, an animal known for eating its own offspring.

Nut's children were two pairs of twins, Osiris and Isis, and Set and Neftis. Osiris and Isis fell in love in their mother's womb, but Neftis hated her brother Set.

As the eldest son of Geb and Nut, Osiris was destined to rule Egypt.

Ra and the Punishment of Humanity

In a text from one of the golden tombs of Tutankhamun's tomb (which reigned between ca. 1336 B.C. and 1327 B.C.), which also appears on the walls of later royal burials, there is talk of a time when Ra, the sun god and creator, lived on earth as the sovereign of gods and men.

When the sun god began to age, humans decided to conspire against him. Seeing this, Ra called upon his divine eye, in the form of the goddess Hathor, as well as Shu, Tefnut, Geb, Nut, and the eight primordial gods of the Ogdoad. Ra sought advice from Nun, the eldest of the eight gods, on what to do with the rebels. Nun and the other gods advised him to send his divine eye to destroy humanity. Ra agreed, and the eye goddess transformed from Hathor to Sekhmet, the roaring lioness, who killed several people and walked among their blood.

The bloodthirsty rampage of Sekhmet was so intense that Ra regretted his decision. To stop her, he ordered thousands of jars of beer to be dyed red with ochre and poured over the fields. Mistaking the beer for blood, Sekhmet drank it until she became drunk and fell asleep. When she awoke, her violent nature had subsided, and she transformed back into Hathor.

Here's the translation of your text into English, rendered in a fluid and engaging style:

Ra was so saddened that he longed to end creation and return to the watery abyss. Nun commanded Shu and Nut to protect the sun god. The sky goddess transformed into a cow and carried Ra into the heavens, where he created the stars and the fields of paradise. Nut staggered from being so high, but Shu and the eight Heh gods held her up.

Every day, the sun god crossed the sky, and each night he entered the underworld. The darkness of night terrified humanity, prompting Ra to create the moon to illuminate the sky during his absence, and appointed Thoth, the moon god, as his delegate. Ra warned the earth god, Geb, about the magical powers of the serpents of chaos and chose Osiris to reign over humanity.

The Egyptians believed this cosmos would not last forever. A time would come when the creator would be so saddened that he and all his works would dissolve into chaos, and then the cycle of creation would begin anew.

Osiris and Isis

The most significant myth to which the Egyptians paid attention and with which they felt the greatest affinity was that of Osiris and his wife and sister, Isis. As is often the case, it's a story of jealousy, the clash of evil against good, the hardships faced by good, and its ultimate triumph over evil, invariably leading to some kind of reward, eternal life, etc.

This theme is a powerful aspect of so many myths from the ancient (and modern) world that it's challenging to pinpoint its origins accurately, although some suggest that Osiris was a god who arrived in Egypt from the Fertile Crescent region in the ancient Near East.

Osiris, the benevolent god, had a jealous brother, Set, who managed to kill him through deceit. To celebrate the return of his brother Osiris from a foreign visit, Set organized a grand feast at the palace, during which Set's servants brought in a magnificently decorated chest. Set proposed that all guests should lie in it, and if anyone fit perfectly, they would receive the splendid object.

Everyone tried, but failed for being too tall, short, fat, or thin (the motif bears some resemblance to the late Greek myth of Theseus and the giant Procrustes, who "fitted" those who slept in his bed by cutting off or stretching their limbs until they fit correctly). In the end, Set convinced his brother Osiris to join the game and measure the chest. Naturally, Osiris fit perfectly in it, as Set had tailored it to his measurements. At a signal from Set, his supporters rushed into the room, forced out Osiris's followers, sealed the chest lid, which became Osiris's coffin, and cast it into the Nile.

The chest containing Osiris's body floated to the sea and appeared on the beach of the city of Byblos, in Lebanon. Reaching near a freshwater spring flowing into the sea, the chest got entangled in the roots of a massive tree, which grew around and enclosed the chest-coffin. The king of Byblos saw the fantastic tree and ordered it to be felled to become the central column of his new palace.

Isis

For the average Egyptian, Isis was the most important deity in their pantheon. She personified all that human life meant and all that was governed by it. She was the "Great Mother," the constant loving wife, the "Queen of Heaven" (a title shared with the Virgin Mary in Christianity), and a faithful protector of family and family values.

She was often depicted as a mother sitting and nursing her young son Horus in her lap. The iconography is very similar to that of Mary and the baby Jesus, which led to numerous religious diatribes among the ancient Christian Church Fathers. Her main temple was located on the island of Philae, near Aswan.

Her cult even survived after the fall of Egyptian civilization, with temples dedicated to her known from Roman times and in remote places of the empire, including Roman London.

Isis in Byblos

The grieving widow, Isis, searched for the chest throughout Egypt; eventually, using her magical powers, she located the body in Byblos. Knowing that the chest and the body were part of the palace, she had to find a way to enter it. Disguising herself as an old woman, she sat by the freshwater stream that flowed to the sea shore, where the maids of the Queen of Byblos came to do laundry. They found her there, pitied the "old lady," brought her food, and treated her kindly. In return, she taught them how to braid their hair, though she couldn't hide her divine scent, and the queen soon noticed the new hairstyles and the fragrance and became curious about these changes. The maids told her about the lonely old lady they had befriended by the sea, who sat there day and night, apparently saddened, though she hadn't told them the cause of her sorrows.

The queen had just given birth to a son and heir and was looking for a nanny. The old lady seemed ideal and was summoned to the palace. Isis (in disguise) accepted the nanny position, on condition that she be left alone with the child at night. Although the queen found this request odd, she consented. At night, the goddess locked herself in the great hall with the child. The maids claimed to hear a strange noise after dark - like the chirping of a bird - and reported it to the queen.

One night, the queen hid behind curtains and, hearing the chirping, stepped out to see her son lying on the hot coals of the fire and a swallow (Isis transformed) flying around the column, making noise. Terrified, the queen took the child in her arms; then, the goddess revealed herself and scolded the queen, accusing her of madness, as she, the goddess, was burning away the child's mortality in the fire.

The king was called, and both monarchs venerated the goddess and asked what they could give her. She demanded the column from the tree trunk enclosing the chest containing her husband's body. Naturally, her request was granted, the roof of the great hall fell, and Isis took Osiris's body back to Egypt and hid it in the marshes of the Delta, where she left it in the care of her sister Neftis.

Osiris

Osiris, brother to the goddesses Isis and Neftis and husband of Isis, became the god of death.

As such, he was one of the most venerated gods of ancient Egypt.

It was by passing through the Hall of Judgment and being presented before him as a just person (ma'at heru - "of true voice") that the deceased could hope for an afterlife.

The Egyptian "heaven" was located in distant western lands, where the sun set: one of Osiris's main titles was "First Lord of the Westerners."

In later times, ushabti figures, meant to work in place of the deceased in the other world, linked the dead to the god and the inscription they bore identified them as "The Osiris N."

Abydos, center of the Osiris cult, was the most sacred place in ancient Egypt, and there Seti I (1291-1278 BC) built the most beautiful of all Egyptian temples.

Osiris: The Defender of Order

On a gold pendant from around 850 BC, Osiris is depicted mummified, flanked by Isis and their son Horus. After his death, Osiris reigned in the underworld (Duat). Initially seen as a fearsome king of a world of demons, he became the just judge welcoming virtuous deceased into paradise.

Osiris, the first king with his sister Isis as consort (see genealogical tree), was worshipped as a god of agriculture, teaching humanity the secrets of farming and civilization. His reign was threatened by the forces of chaos, among them his brother Set. According to a myth, the creation saw discord when Set emerged abruptly from the womb.

The death of the benevolent god Osiris is a pivotal event in Egyptian mythology, but its story is seldom detailed. It encompasses two phases: his murder and dismemberment. Early accounts simply state that Set cast Osiris into the river at

Nedyet, a mythical location sometimes identified with a part of Abydos, the sacred precinct where the mysteries of Osiris were celebrated.

In later versions, Osiris drowned in the Nile, with Set, in the guise of a crocodile or hippopotamus, attacking his innocent brother. In another version, Set transformed into a bull and trampled Osiris to death. Horus later cut off the leg Set used and threw it into the sky, forming part of the Ursa Major constellation. In another tradition, Set, perhaps as a mosquito, fatally stung Osiris in the foot.

Isis searched for her husband and preserved his body using her magical powers. She summoned the jackal god Anubis, who embalmed and wrapped Osiris's body, creating the first mummy. Later myths say Set found Osiris's divine body, dismembered it, and buried the pieces across Egypt: the head in Abydos, the heart in Atribis, a leg on Biga Island, etc. Osiris's dismemberment paralleled the annual harvesting and threshing of wheat and barley. It was believed that the god was reborn with the growth of new seeds.

Isis Returns to Egypt

Motionless above Osiris's body, in the form of a hawk as depicted on the walls of the Osiris sanctuary in the temple of Abydos, Isis became pregnant and in due time gave birth to Horus.

However, Set, the wicked usurper of Osiris's throne, discovered the body while hunting one day in the marshes. Both goddesses were absent, so he cut the body into 14 pieces and scattered them across Egypt. Once again, the grieving widow set out to recover her husband's now dismembered body.

Legend has it that she traveled in a papyrus skiff and, knowing the purpose of her troubled journey, the crocodiles did not attack her (they still don't in modern folk tales, as they evoke the goddess and her quest).

Another version of the myth states that Isis buried each part of her husband's body where she found it, founding a temple there. Another interpretation recounts that she gathered all the parts except one, the phallus, which could not be found because the Oxyrhynchus fish had swallowed it.

After that, the fish was shunned everywhere, except in the city of Oxyrhynchus in the Fayum, where it was considered sacred.

The body (or, according to another version, only the head) was buried in Abydos, which became the most sacred place in ancient Egypt; there, one of the most beautifully decorated temples was built during the reign of Pharaoh Seti I (1291 - 1278 BC).

Typically, each Egyptian temple had seven sanctuaries, dedicated respectively to the king himself, to Ptah, to Ra-Harachte, to Amun-Ra, to Osiris, to Isis, and to Horus.

Anubis, the jackal-headed god, came to Isis's aid after she had gathered 13 parts of the body, and it was he who took care of embalming Osiris's remains. He acted not only as the embalming god but also as a guide of souls, leading them towards the west, the location of the Egyptian "heaven."

Isis Discovers Ra's Secret Name

After the sun god Ra, Isis was the most important Egyptian deity, having discovered Ra's secret name. To know a name meant to have power. Eager for such power, Isis schemed to learn Ra's secret name. As Ra aged, he dozed often, and saliva dripped from his chin. Isis carefully collected some of it and used it to moisten clay with which she formed a venomous snake.

Gods were only vulnerable to something of their own nature, so Isis brought the snake to life and left it where Ra would pass. Naturally, the snake bit him, injecting its venom. Ra was dying from the bite, as, unbeknownst to him, the snake was partly made from Ra's own magical essence, his saliva. Ra trembled with fever and had difficulty speaking. Isis asked him what afflicted him, even though she knew the cause well.

He described his terrible symptoms, and she offered to care for him, but only if he revealed his secret name. He hesitated and gave a list of descriptive names, but she knew none was the secret name. So, she allowed the poison to worsen and asked again for the name. Finally, when he could no longer bear the pain, he agreed to tell her, but only in private and in the absence of other gods.

She had to promise not to tell anyone. After gaining the knowledge she desired, she healed Ra and extracted the venom. Now, knowing the secret name, she had power over him if ever she needed to use it. There was never an occasion to use this knowledge, but she remained satisfied knowing she had such power, should it be necessary.

Isis and Neftis: The Mourning Goddesses

Isis and her sister Neftis, the spouse of Set, watched over their brother Osiris's body in the form of hawks. It was customary for two women to play the roles of Isis and Neftis at funerals and lament in front of the mummified corpse.

Neftis loved Osiris and, according to a late tradition, the god Anubis was their son.

The two goddesses wept for Osiris's death and prayed for his spirit to return.

In one account, Isis declares,

"I will call you as long as I have sight, I will cry to the heavens. You do not come to me, your sister, whom you loved on earth."

In a papyrus dated around 1100 BC, Osiris, the creator god Ptah, and Sokar, a funerary god, appear as a single deity. Isis and Neftis protect his throne.

The animal skin hanging from a post is one of the emblems of Anubis, the god of embalming.

Isis: The Faithful Widow

Isis, consort of Osiris, played an important role in Egyptian mythology from an early period. She rescued her husband's body and used her magical powers to revive him long enough to conceive a child: she transformed into a hawk and, flapping her wings, breathed life into him. According to another version of the myth, Isis became pregnant by a divine fire.

Knowing she was pregnant, Isis fled to the marshes of the Nile delta to hide from her brother Set, who would surely try to harm or even kill the child. She gave birth to a divine son, Horus, near Chemis, close to Buto, and there she raised him, protected by several deities, like Sel-ket, the scorpion goddess, and waited until Horus was old enough to avenge his father.

Her cult spread beyond the borders of Egypt over time. In the late 1st or early 2nd century AD, the Greek Plutarch wrote a version of the Isis and Osiris myth in which Osiris was a king of Egypt who traveled the world teaching humanity agriculture and arts. Set was jealous of his brother and conspired with his followers to dethrone him.

He had a beautiful chest made to Osiris's measurements and during a feast announced he would gift it to whoever fit perfectly inside. Osiris lay in it and found it a perfect fit; Set and the other conspirators nailed the lid shut and sealed it with molten lead. They then threw the coffin into the Nile, which carried it to the Mediterranean and finally to Lebanon. Isis recovered it and took it to Egypt, leaving it only to visit Horus in Buto.

One night, while Isis was away, Set went hunting in the delta and found the coffin. He opened it, divided Osiris's body into fourteen pieces, and scattered them across Egypt. Isis buried each piece where she found it, but couldn't recover the penis, eaten by a fish. This was the primary reason, according to Plutarch, why Egyptian priests did not eat fish.

Isis in Lebanon

Around 100 AD, Plutarch wrote a version of the Isis and Osiris myth in which, upon learning that Set had betrayed and murdered the king, Isis searched everywhere for her husband's body. She went to Byblos, in Lebanon, having heard rumors that it might be there.

The coffin was carried by the waters to Byblos and got caught in the roots of a small tree, which grew so large and beautiful that it was cut down to be used as a pillar in the royal palace of the city. Isis went to the palace and sat in a courtyard, crying.

She won the sympathy of the royal maids by braiding their hair and sprinkling them with perfume, and the Queen of Byblos appointed the goddess as the nanny of her young son. Isis nursed him with a finger instead of her breast and grew so fond of him that she decided to grant him eternal life, placing him on a pyre to consume his mortality.

While the prince lay in the fire, Isis transformed into a swallow and flew around the pillar that had been a tree. The Queen of Byblos heard her laments and entered the room, and seeing her son burning, she screamed, breaking the spell. Isis then revealed her identity and asked that the pillar be cut open. When Osiris's coffin was exposed, Isis let out a wail of pain that caused the prince's death.

Horus and Set

Set had proclaimed himself king, and Isis, now with her young son Horus, went into hiding. When

Horus reached manhood, he challenged his evil uncle Set to regain his father's throne. The various battles between them, known as the Contests of Horus and Set, are depicted and illustrated in lengthy texts and reliefs on the walls of the temple of Horus in Edfu - one of the best-preserved and complete temples of ancient Egypt.

In the carvings of the two gods fighting, Set is often depicted as a small male hippopotamus being wounded by Horus's long spear. (While the male hippopotamus embodied evil in ancient Egypt, the female was associated with the goddess Taweret and highly revered by women as a protector of childbirth.)

At one point, when Set found Horus sleeping in the desert (Set's domain), he blinded him, the eyes symbolizing the sun and the moon in mythology. However, the goddess Hathor (often assimilated with Isis in later Egyptian mythology) restored his sight by washing the damaged eyes with gazelle milk.

The Eye of Horus (the udjat) became one of the most powerful protective amulets in Egypt; children wore it around their necks or on a bracelet and set in beautiful jewelry, like the one found in the mummy of the young pharaoh Tutankhamun.

Horus

Horus, son of Osiris and Isis, was regarded as the obedient son who avenged his father's murder.

The Pharaoh on earth identified with this god: the third of the five names of the Pharaoh was the "Golden Horus Name," and he was called the "Living Horus."

As a falcon god, he was the Lord of the Sky and took the form of a bird, but he could also be seen as a small child nursing in the lap of his mother Isis.

His main temple was at Edfu, south of Luxor, one of the best-preserved temples of ancient Egypt, although its current structure dates to the Ptolemaic (Greek) period of Egyptian civilization.

Horus and Set: The Struggle for Osiris's Throne

The conflict between Horus and Set, often violent, is a fundamental element of Egyptian mythology. In early versions of this myth, Set and Horus appear as brothers, but later they were considered uncle and nephew. After his brother Osiris's death, Horus's father, Set seized the throne, and Horus appealed to a divine tribunal presided over by Geb or Ra for succession. Shu and Thoth declared that it was Horus, not Set, who had the right to rule.

The sun god was angered because his opinion had not been sought and refused to accept the judgment. One of the gods insulted him, and the sun god withdrew to his tent, sulking. Later, in a better mood, he told Set and Horus to defend their claims themselves. Set claimed he deserved to be king because only he had enough strength to defend the sun's boat. Several members of the Ennead supported him, but Isis convinced them to change their minds.

Set refused to continue the trial in Isis's presence, and the sun god agreed to meet the council on an island. The divine ferryman, Nemti, was ordered not to take Isis, but she disguised herself as an old woman and bribed Nemti with a gold ring. Arriving on the island, she transformed into a beautiful young woman to entice Set and sought his help: she told him she was the widow of a herdsman and a stranger had robbed her son of his cattle. Set responded that it was a real injustice for a boy to be deprived of his father's inheritance. Isis immediately transformed into a hawk and flew to the top of a tree, where she told Set he had condemned himself with his own words.

Set complained to the Ennead about this incident, and the nine gods cut off Nemti's toes as punishment. Set challenged Horus to a test of strength, in which both would turn into hippos and try to stay underwater for three months. Horus agreed, but as Isis feared her son would lose, she made a copper harpoon and threw it into the water. First, she accidentally hit Horus and then Set, who begged for mercy.

The goddess took pity on him and let him go. Enraged, Horus emerged from the water, cut off his mother's head, and fled with it to the desert mountains. Isis turned into a stone statue to disguise herself and returned to the assembly of gods, but Thoth recognized her. The sun god ordered the Ennead to punish Horus for what he had done to his mother. Later, Set found him sleeping and removed his eyes, but the goddess Hathor restored the young god's sight with gazelle milk.

After Horus again sought justice, the gods wrote a letter to the deceased Osiris, who replied asking why his son had been deprived of his inheritance and threatened to send the demons of the underworld to the realm of the gods. The sun king finally agreed that Horus should be king, forced Set to accept the verdict, and Isis rejoiced to see her son crowned. The sun god called Set to live with him in heaven and made him the god of storms.

The Eye of Horus

In a faience amulet, the Eye of Horus or Wadjet is depicted: the Complete One.

As the god of the sky, Horus took the form of a falcon: his right eye was the sun and the left eye the moon.

During a terrible fight, Horus wounded Set in the testicles, and Set injured Horus in one or both eyes. According to another version, Set, in the form of a black pig, tore out and swallowed Horus's moon eye

Followers of Set

The Egyptians depicted Set as a mythical animal, part wild donkey and part pig or aardvark.

His domains were the desert and he was associated with most animals from this region, like oxen and donkeys, because they were used for barley threshing and trampled the body of Set's victim, Osiris, Horus's father, found in the grain.

Horus condemned these beasts to be eternally beaten. A series of myths in northern Upper Egypt deal with conflicts between the human followers of Set and the allies of Horus.

Set continually attempted to mistreat Osiris's body by taking the form of various animals. Once he transformed into a panther, but Thoth recited magical incantations against him and Set fell to the ground.

Anubis tied him up, branded him with iron, and skinned him. His followers tried to rescue him, but Anubis beheaded them.

Set recovered from his injuries and gathered other followers in the desert mountains, but Isis turned against him. Set transformed into a bull, Isis into a dog with a knife at the end of its tail and chased him, and the goddess Hathor into a venomous snake that bit Set's followers, whose blood stained the mountains red.

Set, the strongest of the gods, defended the solar boat from the serpent Apep.

Solar Myth: The Eternal Cycle of Renewal

The sun god was the primary deity in Egypt in most periods. The world was organized according to two interdependent principles: the appearance and actions of the creator and the daily cycle of the sun through the cosmos, a cosmos that, essentially, was identified with Egypt.

Every day, at dawn, the sun god was born from the sky goddess. He reached maturity at midday, old age in the afternoon, and at nightfall entered the underworld. Each day, month, and year, as well as each monarch's reign, renewed the world's creation, and this constant renewal implied a continuous threat, a pessimistic view appearing in cycles of hymns to the sun god and in compositions describing his transit through the underworld, all aimed at maintaining the order of things. The god traveled in a boat and was served by countless beings, including the blessed dead. Only a few were depicted, aspects of the sun god's being or deities leading and defending the boat. The god's eternal adversaries, led by the giant serpent Apep, tried to prevent his journey through the sky and the underworld.

The entire creation hailed the birth of the sun, and this welcome supported the sun god's transit. Some traditions focused on the god's essential benevolence, and the texts that presented him in this light provided the starting point for the monotheistic religious ideas of Pharaoh Akhenaten.

Sun God, Nightly Journey, and the Stars

The ancients believed that the sun god traversed the underworld during his nightly journey, depicted in the extensive Books of the Underworld inscribed in royal tombs of the New Kingdom so that the Pharaoh could join the solar cycle in the afterlife.

These Books of the Underworld are divided into the twelve hours of the night, each focusing on the sun god in his boat, surrounded by the beings inhabiting that region. One composition features about a thousand figures: the blessed dead, demons and deities of the region, and the damned enduring endless torment. As the sun god passes, he greets the beings of each hour, who welcome him and are revived by the light radiating from the deity.

The descriptions are highly detailed, providing dimensions of the spaces traversed. His boat typically sails a waterway but at times moves across endless sands, pulled by a pack of jackals.

Some compositions depict the sun god, at midnight, descending to the deepest regions of the underworld and merging with its lord, Osiris. The image bears the legends "Ra, resting in Osiris" and "Osiris, resting in Ra." While Ra could be linked with Amun to form a single deity (Amun-Ra), Ra and Osiris had fundamental differences. Their brief association led to daily renewal, but it wasn't permanent.

The sun god had to battle his worst enemy, the serpent Apep, throughout the night, but in the final hours, he entered a serpent from which he emerged rejuvenated and reborn at dawn. The solar cycle was commemorated daily in many temples, not just in solar sanctuaries. The priests conducted the rituals inside the building, with little known about them outside.

The core elements of the worship were kept secret and are known from certain records dating from 1100 BC and later. The ultimate meaning of much of the solar cycle was hidden. A text states that the Pharaoh, as high priest, "knows" eight things about the rising sun, including the "words spoken by the Souls of the East," the baboons, animals that often scream at dawn. Only the Pharaoh knew the hidden meaning of their cries.

The sun god took multiple forms during his daily cycle. As the morning god, he could be a child, but usually was a scarab, Khepri. This beetle, pushing a dung ball akin to the sun, symbolized regeneration, rebirth, and transformation. At noon, the sun god was Herakhty-Ra, "Ra, Horus of the Horizon," often depicted as a human figure with a falcon head topped by a solar disk. Herakhty was an ancient god, and the idea of a falcon crossing the sky in a boat dates back to the 1st Dynasty. Herakhty-Ra was the most common name in myths about the god's role on earth.

The evening sun was Aten or Aten-Ra, in human form with the double crown worn by Pharaohs. His nocturnal form, with a ram's head, was simply a pictorial figure without a specific name, but was called "Flesh (of Ra)," implying the image was a vessel for the sun god's presence without strictly identifying with him.

There were other gods associated with the heavens, and some major deities linked to stars or planets: Thoth was the Moon; Set, Mercury; and Osiris, the Orion constellation. The myths of the Ennead were represented in the complex movements of celestial bodies, especially those crossing the sun's path or, like Venus, heralding dawn.

Secret Name of Ra: Book of Thoth

For the Egyptians, magic held great value in this world and the next, as a means to foresee and prevent misfortunes. Some magical spells, which recounted mythical episodes, were recited as a patient, identified with the myth's protagonist, consumed medicine or received body applications. Magical hymns directed at gods, whose real names were kept secret for their magical power, were part of this.

One tale, part of these magical spells, narrates how Isis discovered the most secret divine name of the sun god Ra. As Ra grew old and sometimes drooled, Isis saw where his saliva fell, mixed it with clay, and formed a serpent, which she brought to life and left along Ra's usual walking path.

When Ra passed by, the serpent bit him and vanished. Ra instantly felt immense pain as the venom spread through his body. He called the nine gods, telling them he was wounded by something he hadn't created. Isis promised to cure him if he revealed his true name. Ra listed names he was known by at different times of day, but Isis insisted these weren't his true name.

As the pain worsened and Ra couldn't bear it, he confided his secret name to Isis. She then drew out the venom using Ra's true name, curing him and promising not to share the power of the secret name with anyone, except Horus. The spell does not reveal the name.

Bes was one of the many monstrous-looking deities that protected from misfortunes. His image appeared in various ornamental motifs, especially on small domestic items or amulets used for protection. Bes, with his distinctive and fearsome appearance, was a common figure in ancient Egyptian art, symbolizing protection and warding off evil.

The Magic of Thoth

Thoth, the moon god, depicted as a baboon, ibis, or a man with an ibis head, had a special connection with the secret knowledge of magic. His main worship center was at Khemenu (Heliopolis to the Greeks), where he was identified with Hermes. In a Ptolemaic era story, a prince named Setna Khaemuese hears about a magical book by Thoth buried in a tomb near Memphis. Despite warnings, Setna retrieves the book but encounters a seductive phantom, leading to a series of illusions and realizations. This teaches him a lesson, prompting him to return the book of Thoth.

Serpents and Scorpions

Serpents and scorpions were more than just everyday dangers; they embodied the chaotic powers threatening the world order. A literary text describes a government official's encounter with a giant serpent, possibly with a human head, on a fabulous island after a shipwreck. The serpent shares its own tragic story, adding a moral about enduring losses. The number 74, mentioned in the story, refers to the 74 manifestations of the sun god consumed in the final holocaust of creation. The serpent's form exists in a realm beyond creation, placing the traveler outside of time. Mastery over serpents and scorpions was beneficial. The principal scorpion goddess was Selket, protector of births and mummified bodies. Other snake goddesses like Renenet and Mertseger were associated with specific locations.

The story of Thoth's magic captivates with its blend of mystery and enchantment. Thoth, the moon god, revered for his wisdom and connection to the arcane, was worshipped prominently in Khemenu. In an intriguing tale from the Ptolemaic era, Prince Setna Khaemuese is lured by the legend of Thoth's magical book. His journey leads him to a ghostly encounter and a series of transformative illusions, culminating in a lesson about the pursuit of forbidden knowledge and the need for respect towards the mystical.

Serpents and scorpions, more than mere threats, symbolize chaotic forces in the Egyptian cosmos. A narrative involving a government official and a mystical serpent on a fantastical island delves into themes of loss and cosmic order. The serpent, linked to the sun god's 74 manifestations, represents a realm beyond conventional existence. The story elegantly intertwines mythology with moral lessons, illustrating the profound impact of serpents and scorpions in Egyptian lore, where they were revered and feared.

Spells for Healing Poisoning

Numerous magical spells existed to combat wounds from snakes and scorpions, which couldn't be treated medically. Some included mythological stories featuring these creatures. In one such tale, Isis, fleeing from Set's workshop, heads to Chemis with seven discreet scorpions to secretly raise Horus. A rich woman's refusal to shelter them leads to her son being stung, but Isis intervenes, saving the child and teaching a moral lesson about generosity and the rewards of kindness, particularly among the poor and marginalized.

This story underlines that extraordinary events can disrupt the natural order and implies that even the sun's appearance and seasons might be affected if certain magical outcomes are not achieved.

Neith

Neith, the Great Mother and a prominent war and hunting deity, was feared for her capacity to unleash war or destruction. Her saliva is said to have created Apep, the chaos serpent. Neith's advice in the Horus and Set conflict was so pivotal that she threatened to collapse the sky if her recommendations were not followed.

Sekhmet and Bast

Sekhmet, a formidable lioness goddess, was tasked by the sun god to annihilate rebellious humanity and was sometimes appeased through sacrifices. She was associated with contagious diseases, with her priests acting as healers. Bast, initially a lioness deity, evolved into a cat goddess representing love, sex, and fertility, highlighting the diverse and influential nature of feline deities in Egyptian mythology.

The Cat and the Lioness

In this myth, the Eye of Ra, associated with the goddess Hathor, flees to Nubia, south of Egypt. The story showcases the Eye of Ra in two feline forms:

Sekhmet, the lioness goddess, and Bast, the cat goddess. Upset with her father, the Eye of Ra retreats to Nubia. Thoth, disguised as a baboon, follows and encounters her as a cat goddess. He shares stories to calm her and entices her back to Egypt with promises of temple offerings. Despite an assassination attempt by a chaos serpent near Thebes, Thoth saves her and she reunites with Ra in Heliópolis, transforming into Hathor. A bronze figure from the Late Period shows Bast with kittens, symbolizing her role as a fertility deity, celebrated annually in Bubastis.

Anat

In a letter during Horus and Set's conflict, Neith suggests giving Set two foreign goddesses, Anat and Astarte, as compensation for ceding his throne rights to Horus, possibly implying Set wasn't worthy of an Egyptian goddess. In another narrative, Set assaults Hathor in the river and becomes ill, as Hathor was the consort of the nocturnal sun and only divine prayer could impregnate her. Set's wife Anat seeks Ra's help, and Isis retrieves the divine seed, healing Set.

Astarte and Taweret

Astarte

Astarte, another of Set's foreign wives, features in a myth where the Egyptian gods face off against the sea deity. Ptah and the Ennead were forced to pay tribute to the sea. Renenutet brought gold, silver, and lapis lazuli to the shore, but the insatiable sea demanded more, threatening to enslave the Egyptian gods. Renenutet sent a bird to Astarte's house, urging her to appease the sea with her tribute. Astarte wept but eventually brought her tribute to the shore. Upon arrival, she mockingly sang to the sea, which then demanded Astarte herself. The cunning goddess appeared before the Ennead, who adorned her with several jewels, including Nut's necklace and Geb's seal. Astarte, accompanied by a battle-ready Set, went to the shore to confront the sea. The story's ending is lost, but it likely concludes with Set overcoming the sea and saving Astarte.

Foreign Goddesses in Egypt

By the end of the 2nd millennium BC, several Syrian and Palestinian goddesses were assimilated into the Egyptian pantheon, including:

- Anat: A warrior goddess typically depicted with a shield, spear, and axe. In Syria, she was Baal's sister and lover, worshipped in Egypt as Set. In

Egyptian mythology, Anat was Ra's daughter. She dressed as a male warrior but was also revered as a cow goddess.

- Astarte: Another warrior goddess, akin to Mesopotamia's Ishtar. In Egypt, she was the sun god's or Ptah's daughter, often depicted as a nude woman with weapons or as a horse.

- Kudshu: Consort of Min, the Egyptian fertility god, sometimes depicted as Hathor. She appeared as a nude woman on a lion, with snakes and lotus flowers.

Hathor and Taweret

Hathor, the protector of lovers, was one of the most complex Egyptian deities, with her main temple at Dendera. Like Taweret, she guarded women and children and was linked to death and rebirth. Hathor assisted women in conceiving and childbirth, raising Horus as a cow in Chemis. She welcomed souls in the underworld, offering them food and drink. Taweret, helping the dead to be reborn in the Nun, could appear as a formidable beast, part hippopotamus, part lion, and part crocodile. Sometimes considered Set's consort due to her hippopotamus form, Taweret prevented further harm when Set's leg was cast into the sky. Both Hathor and Taweret, symbolized by a divine cow, were linked to the Great Flood at the underworld's entrance in the mountains west of Thebes, as depicted in the Book of the Dead.

The Sacred Role of the Pharaohs

Upon ascending the throne, the Egyptian Pharaoh became a god, embodying Horus, the sky god, and son of Ra, the sun god. Protected by Nekhbet and Uadjet, goddesses of Upper and Lower Egypt, his titles expressed these divine connections. Each Pharaoh's unique throne name declared their manifestation of the sun god, like Tutmosis IV's "Menkheprura" meaning "Enduring are the Manifestations of Ra." The Pharaoh could be the "son" of any major deity, transcending mere divine offspring status. This divine lineage was extended to the Pharaoh being nursed by goddesses as a child, and numerous tales depicted the monarch as a descendant of the sun god. In these stories, the reigning Pharaoh engaged with the mother of his successor, conceiving a child recognized by the god's scent. The creator god Khnum shaped the child on his potter's wheel, and childbirth was attended by numerous deities, with divine blessings and nursing by goddesses. Some Pharaohs transcended their traditional role and were deified in life, like Amenhotep III, while others, like Senuosret III and Amenemhat III, were worshipped posthumously as local deities.

Rudjedet and Khuíiu

The divine origin myth of the Pharaohs intertwined with historical events. A papyrus recounts the birth and survival of the first three Pharaohs of the 5th Dynasty. Rudjedet, wife of a priest, bore triplets fathered by Ra, with Isis, Neftis, and other deities protecting her from Khufu, the 4th Dynasty Pharaoh. Disguised as musicians, the deities attended the birth, named the children, and left three crowns as symbols of royalty. Later, a dispute with a servant led to an attempt to betray Rudjedet to Khufu, but divine crocodiles, agents of divine punishment, intervened, ensuring the children's survival and succession to Khufu's throne.

The tale of Rudjedet and her triplets, fathered by the sun god Ra, continues with a dramatic turn. Rudjedet's conflict with her servant leads to an attempted betrayal. However, divine intervention in the form of crocodiles, representing agents of divine retribution, saves the day. This action ensures the safety of the children, who are destined to succeed Khufu as rulers. This story elegantly blends the themes of divine lineage, protection, and the inevitable ascension of divinely chosen rulers in ancient Egyptian mythology.

Gods and Humans

In Egyptian mythology, the interactions between gods and humans are relatively rare. One late 2nd millennium BC story involves two brothers, Anubis (the jackal god) and Bata (a bull god, an aspect of Set), both bearing the names of gods. Bata, possessing extraordinary strength and able to understand animals, lives with his older brother Anubis, assisting in farming and cattle herding. One day, a series of events leads Bata to confront and refuse the seductive advances of Anubis's wife. Fearing Bata would tell Anubis, she feigns an attack by Bata. Anubis, enraged, attempts to kill Bata, who prays to the sun god for protection. A river filled with crocodiles separates them, and Bata castrates himself to prove his innocence. Anubis believes him and kills his wife.

Bata then moves to the Valley of the Pine in Syria, where he hides his heart in a pine tree and builds a mansion. The gods, pitying his loneliness, create a divine wife for him. However, her fate is predicted to be tragic. Bata warns her not to leave the house, but she disobeys, leading to her hair being taken to Egypt and discovered by the Pharaoh's launderers. Enchanted by its beauty and scent, the Pharaoh searches for its owner. Bata defends his valley but is ultimately betrayed when his wife reveals the secret of his heart. The pine is cut down, Bata dies, and his wife becomes the Pharaoh's favorite.

Anubis discovers his deceased brother Bata and, after a long search, revives him using his dried heart. Bata, transformed into a magnificent bull, asks Anubis to gift him to the Pharaoh. At court, Bata reveals his identity to the queen. Later, she manipulates the Pharaoh into sacrificing the bull for his liver. From Bata's dying blood, two beautiful persea trees grow, which the queen recognizes as Bata and orders to be made into furniture. Swallowing a splinter from the wood, she becomes pregnant, giving birth to a son who eventually declares himself as Bata, recounts his story, orders the queen's execution, and rules for thirty years before being succeeded by Anubis.

Gods with Human Forms in Egypt

All the previous deities were from the heavens. More popular among the Egyptians, and better known to posterity, were the divinities of the earth. Among these, the most important were those that make up the triad Osiris, Isis, and Horus, which form a human legend similar to the fables of Greece and Rome.

What is the origin of this legend?

Fre incarnated in Osiris, descended to the earth, and he and his descendants (the Osirians) reigned for thirty thousand years.

Osiris is credited with the conquest and civilization of the Nile Valley. Osiris invented sciences and arts and communicated them to mankind. Osiris is the prototype of the benevolent monarch. And he was always accompanied by Thoth, the sacred writer and confidant, the high priest of the Osirian cult.

Osiris's wife and sister was Isis. Their children were Macedo and Anubis. The son of Osiris and Isis was Horus. Osiris set out to conquer, accompanied by Anubis and Macedo; ruling Egypt, he left Isis in charge, advised by Thoth and Djom (the Egyptian Hercules). For the Greeks, Osiris was the brother of Apollo. Osiris subdued all of Ethiopia, channeled the Nile River, crossed Arabia, and reached India. In Thrace, after killing the king, he established Maron in the western basket, where he built the city of Marenea, and left Macedo in a region that was named Macedonia after him.

In his absence, Typhon, the god of evil and Osiris's brother, had tried to seize Egypt. But sometimes the advice of Thoth thwarted the plot, and at other times the determination of Djom forced Typhon to give up his attempts. And in Egypt, Typhon invited Osiris to a grand banquet, during which he managed to lock Osiris in a chest and throw it into the Nile, through whose mouth Tanita gave the chest to the sea. The adventures of Isis to find the chest were great and even greater. Once she possessed the body of her beloved husband, she had Anubis embalm him, and she went to visit the goddess Buto, the godmother and nurse of Horus.

Again, Typhon found his brother's body; he tore it into fourteen pieces and threw them to as many points on the island of the Delta. Once again, the grieving Isis set out to find those beloved pieces by the seven mouths of the Nile, but she could only find thirteen pieces; the generative organ was missing, eaten by the fish called lepidotes and oxirrincos, cursed ever since. Horus, immortalized by Hato, now grown, fought and defeated Typhon and his accomplices, reclaiming the Egyptian crown.

Isis, the second divinity of the earthly triad, becomes what among the heavenly divinities are Bulo, Athor, Neith, and Pooh, and in her role as the great mother, she breastfeeds her son Horus.

If Osiris represents the fertile Nile, Isis symbolizes the fertile land; if Osiris is the Sun, Isis is the Moon, receiving light and influence from that celestial body.

Horus, also called Uro, Or, Ar, was the third divinity of the earthly triad. As the avenger and successor of his father, he was regarded as Osiris himself and received the same honors in that regard.

Osiris was the dying Sun - every day; Horus, the Sun that is born every day. The Greeks, who regarded Horus as their god Apollo, gave that god a twin sister, Bubastis, similar to Artemis, Apollo's twin sister. Anubis was the child of an involuntary union between Osiris and Nef-te, the spouse of Typhon. The compassionate Isis forgave Osiris and adopted Anubis, raising him alongside Horus.

Anubis, for embalming Osiris' body, was considered the god overseeing the transition from life to death. When the supreme moment arrived for the soul to leave its body, Anubis placed the body in a coffin and guided the soul to the silent and fantastical realms of Amenti. Anubis resided in the fateful reed that separated the realm of light from the kingdom of shadows and was symbolized by a dog's head due to his faithfulness in guarding. Macedo, another son of Osiris, had the head of a wolf and led Osiris' army in the vanguard, symbolizing impetuosity. Anubis was in the rearguard, symbolizing vigilance.

Typhon, Osiris and Isis' brother, personified all that was disastrous or malevolent. Physically, he represented extreme weakness and all forms of monstrosity or deformity. Morally, he epitomized vice, envy, ambition, hypocrisy, rebellion, and slander. The Egyptians believed he was the immense and dark sea that swallowed the fertile waters of the sacred Nile. Animals like the wild boar and scorpion were dedicated to him, as their appearances were associated with his misdeeds. For instance, the crocodile, since it transformed into a fearsome reptile to escape Horus' revenge.

Thoth, an emanation of the celestial Thoth I mentioned earlier, was an earthly deity, the prototype of the priest and the sage. He gave Isis the cow's horns as a replacement for the diadem that Horus had taken from her. Thoth was credited with the invention of arithmetic and the alphabet, as well as music, trade, currency, and the three-stringed lyre.

Djom, who represented the execution of justice among celestial deities, played an eminently warrior role among terrestrial deities. As the Egyptian Hercules, he was responsible for maintaining peace and defending the land against the enemies of the gods. Sate or Na was the goddess of truth and justice.

Suan, the goddess of childbirth; Besa, the goddess of oracles given through sealed letters.

Salete, the goddess and daughter of the Nile; Ambo, the subterranean Isis, the goddess of the underworld; Anuke, a symbol of celestial fire.

In this way, the Egyptian people, who began by worshiping a single god, then multiplied their gods, even adoring animals and plants, returned to the starting point of their beliefs, worshiping once again a single god that summarized and condensed their past idolatries.

Setna Khaemwese and Imhotep

The "ba" was the spiritual aspect of an individual, usually represented as a bird with a human head. The "ba" of a deceased person could move through the underworld and return to the land of the living during the day.

Typically, the human heroes in Egyptian stories are not warriors but rather magicians or master-priests, men who studied the books of magic kept in temples.

In a papyrus dated to the mid-2nd millennium BCE, several tales of their magical exploits are recorded. For instance, a master-priest brought a wax crocodile to life to kill his wife's lover, and another magician, a simple villager, tamed a lion and reattached the head of a decapitated goose.

The cycle of stories about Prince Setna Khaemwese, from a later period, recounts the rivalry between the priest-magicians of Egypt and the sorcerers from Nubia. The real Setna Khaemwese was the son of Ramses II (circa 1279-1213 BCE) and, as the high priest of Ptah, he studied and restored several pyramids and tombs in Giza, which likely earned him a reputation as a magician.

According to this cycle, a Nubian chief challenges the pharaoh to find a man capable of reading a sealed letter. Siosire, the young son of Setna, accomplishes this feat, and the letter reveals the following: "Long ago, a sorcerer of a Nubian king brought four wax figures to life, kidnapped the Egyptian monarch, and subjected him to five hundred lashes before returning him to his palace.

The humiliation was avenged by an Egyptian named Horus, the son of Paneshe, who treated the Nubian king in the same way and then defeated the Nubian sorcerer in a magic competition, banishing him from Egypt for 1,500 years."

After reading the letter, the Nubian chief declares that he is the sorcerer who has returned for revenge. Siosire reveals that he is Horus, the son of Paneshe. The Egyptian defeats the Nubian and returns to the underworld.

Imhotep and the Seven-Year Famine

In myths, a real person appears, Imhotep, who was the minister and architect of Pharaoh Djoser in the 27th century BCE.

According to tradition, he was the son of Ptah and a woman. The following story comes from an inscription near Aswan, supposedly a decree by Djoser, but it was actually written by the priests of Khnum around the 2nd century BCE.

For seven years, the Nile did not rise enough to irrigate the fields.

As Pharaoh Djoser's subjects were on the brink of starving, the monarch consulted Imhotep, the chief master-priest, about the cause of the insufficient flooding. Imhotep discovered that Hapi, the spirit of the inundation, lived in twin caves beneath the island of Elephantine.

When the time of flooding came, the gates were held closed by the ram-headed god Khnum, who could open the doors of the caves. Upon hearing this, Djoser made generous offerings to Khnum, and that night, in a dream, the god promised the pharaoh that he would release Hapi. An abundant harvest ended the famine.

Imhotep is also credited with inventing stone architecture and writing books of wisdom. Long after his death, he was revered as the god of medicine.

Life After Death

The Soul in the Underworld

In the episode from the Setna cycle, Siosire takes his father to the underworld to show him the fate of two men after they have died and been judged by Osiris: one, a cruel and wealthy man, is condemned to eternal torment, and the other, poor and virtuous, has been granted all the burial objects of the rich man and is a blessed spirit.

In this late text, the judgment of the dead is presented as a central element of Egyptian religion. In earlier times, it was one of the many dangers the soul had to overcome upon reaching the paradise known as the Field of Reeds.

The Egyptians imagined the underworld as a complex landscape of rivers and islands, deserts and lakes of fire. To gain access to it or to appease and overcome the gods and demons who inhabited it, the soul had to become a hero-magician.

Starting in the late 3rd millennium BCE, spells were inscribed on the coffins of wealthy and high-ranking individuals, and later, these spells became part of a body of texts called the Book of the Dead.

From the 16th century BCE, rolls of papyrus with illustrated selections from this book were buried alongside wealthy Egyptians. The deceased were depicted overcoming the dangers of the underworld, such as the four crocodiles of the West.

Upon entering the throne room of Osiris, the deceased had to declare themselves innocent of various crimes before the forty-two judges of the underworld. The heart (i.e., the conscience) was weighed on a scale, with the counterweight being the feather of the goddess Maat, the personification of justice and truth.

A female monster, the Devourer of the Dead, crouched beside the scale, ready to devour the deceased if the heart weighed more than the feather.

Such a fate could be avoided by using a spell that prevented the heart from confessing the sins committed by its owner. Those who passed the test were deemed pure and became spirits with the power to move among the gods, and in some cases, they were invited to join the millions of beings who traveled on the solar barque and battled Apep, the serpent of chaos.

Eternal Echoes: The Gods of Egypt and the Human Spirit

"The gods of Egypt, with their rich and intricate mythologies, hold a unique place in the annals of human history. These divine beings, often depicted with animal heads atop human bodies, were not mere superstitions but rather complex symbols of the Egyptian worldview.

Their stories, passed down through generations, served as a cultural tapestry that wove together the beliefs, values, and aspirations of a civilization that thrived along the banks of the Nile. These tales offered not just a glimpse into the pantheon of gods but also a profound exploration of human nature.

The concept of life after death, central to Egyptian spirituality, found expression in the elaborate rituals and spells, inscribed in texts like the Book of the Dead, that guided souls through the perilous journey of the afterlife. The heart, symbolizing one's conscience, was weighed against the feather of Maat, the goddess of truth and justice, in the presence of Osiris, the god of the afterlife. This judgment was a reflection of the Egyptian belief in moral accountability, where one's deeds in life determined their fate in death.

Moreover, the gods of Egypt were not distant deities but interactive beings who influenced the daily lives of the people. Offerings, prayers, and festivals were dedicated to these gods to seek their favor and protection. Each god or goddess represented different aspects of life, from the nurturing Hathor to the fierce Sekhmet, highlighting the diversity and depth of Egyptian spirituality.

The Egyptian cosmos was not just a physical realm but also a battleground of cosmic forces. The eternal struggle between order (represented by gods like Ra and Horus) and chaos (embodied by the serpent Apep) was a recurring theme. This cosmic battle mirrored the challenges of maintaining harmony and stability in the natural and social order.

In conclusion, the gods of Egypt are not relics of the past but timeless symbols that continue to fascinate and inspire. They offer a profound reflection on the human condition, our quest for meaning, and the enduring mysteries that unite us across cultures and eras. As we delve into the stories of Osiris, Isis, Anubis, and others, we embark on a journey through the heart of ancient Egypt's spiritual landscape, where the divine and mortal realms intertwine, revealing insights into the beliefs and aspirations of a civilization that spanned millennia."